The Simon

For Peter Lewis, who encouraged
me to write about another Peter.

The
Simon Peter file
Renewal comes
to Canwell Park

Derek Wood

Inter-Varsity Press

INTER-VARSITY PRESS
38 De Montfort Street, Leicester LE1 7GP, England

© Derek Wood, 1989

Unless otherwise stated, Scripture quotations in this publication are from the Holy Bible, New International Version. Copyright © 1973, 1978, 1984 International Bible Society. Published by Hodder & Stoughton.

First published 1989

British Library Cataloguing in Publication Data
Wood, Derek, 1934-
    The Simon Peter file: renewal comes to Canwell Park
    1. Christian life. Personal observations
    I. Title
    248.4

ISBN 0-85110-847-4

Set in Clearface
Typeset in Great Britain by Emset, London NW10.
Printed and bound in Great Britain by BPCC Hazell Books Ltd
Member of BPCC Ltd, Aylesbury, Bucks, England

Inter-Varsity Press is the book-publishing division of the Universities and Colleges Christian Fellowship (formerly the Inter-Varsity Fellowship), a student movement linking Christian Unions in universities and colleges throughout the United Kingdom and the Republic of Ireland, and a member movement of the International Fellowship of Evangelical Students. For information about local and national activities write to UCCF, 38 De Montfort Street, Leicester LE1 7GP.

Contents

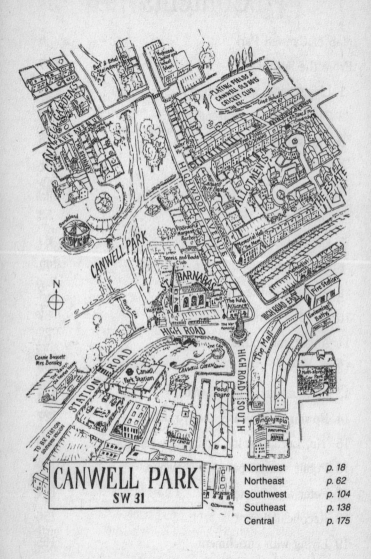

CANWELL PARK
SW 31

From the author

Welcome back to Canwell Park, SW31!

The encouragement described in *The Barnabas factor* has blossomed into new life in the Spirit at St Barnabas'. For some. Others are resentful and suspicious. Extreme positions are taken up and encouragement is forgotten in conflict.

In my experience this is not untypical of church life today. Why? Why must we see everything in black and white and act so intolerantly to our brothers and sisters? Two vital ingredients are often lacking.

Lack of love is the first. It is no coincidence that Paul's great ode to self-giving love (1 Corinthians 13) is sandwiched between chapters on spiritual gifts and worship.

Lack of understanding is the other: understanding that the truth often lies somewhere between our extreme positions, and sometimes *in both extremes at once*. This is paradox, mystery, apparent contradiction. We can't cope. This is where Simon Peter comes in. He above every other Bible character is a contradiction walking on two legs; bold yet timid, self-confident yet collapsing like a pricked balloon, the mouthpiece of God yet a messenger for Satan, capable of violent swings of emotion. Good old Peter! But what a *frustrating* man to have to work with.

The Simon Peter File traces the parallel stories of Simon Peter and the Canwell Park congregation. I hope you will enjoy both. If along the way you become a little more tolerant, loving and understanding, that will make me very happy. But it will make you even happier.

My grateful thanks to all who have helped in the birth of this book, not least to those whose ideas I have borrowed without detailed acknowledgment, and also to Marie Palmer who finished typing the manuscript and then produced her first baby! To the Christian church, absurd yet loving, inconsistent yet forgiving, intolerant yet accepting even me, thank you.

Derek Wood

1
Living with contradictions

Timothy Monteith, vicar of St Barnabas' Church, Canwell Park, London SW31, took a deep breath, then another, prayed a short prayer, grasped the handle and opened his front door. He walked with purposeful tread across the car park to the church hall. The church council was to meet at 7.45.

He wondered, as he walked the fifty yards or so, why it is that church council meetings seem to bring out the worst in people. Good, honest, Christian people who get on well together in ordinary circumstances, seem to divide themselves into factions for no apparent reason. Some, usually businessmen, take the line that it is their responsibility to keep the minister on the right track, not allow him too much rope. That means opposing every idea he ever has. Others seem to think that the meetings are intended for discussion of the furniture, the drain-pipes, the kitchen equipment and the cutting of the graveyard grass, but not the kingdom of God.

Still others raise their eyebrows in despair when such mundane and unspiritual matters are in view and make remarks about the worldliness of the church. Some talk too much. Others say nothing whatever, in the meeting, but complain bitterly afterwards about the decisions made and the ones that should have been made. And the vicar has to be chairman!

As if all that were not enough, there was Item Six. Item Six on the agenda was the proposal that the church pews should be removed to allow for 'greater freedom of worship'. Behind that was the desire of some of the members to 'speed up the growth of encouragement' (as they put it) or to 'go wildly charismatic' (as their opponents preferred to say). The church had grown recently, not only in numbers but also in warmth and openness and in members being more deeply committed to God and to each other. A series of sermons on Barnabas, the 'son of encouragement', and a number of out-of-the-way happenings (chronicled in *The Barnabas Factor*) had opened the way to this growth, but suddenly events had taken a new twist and now the church faced division and conflict. Why did it have to happen to him? Timothy had not supported one side or the other, yet now the battle lines were being drawn and church members were converging on the hall from every corner of Canwell Park and Item Six would still be on the agenda whether he wished it away or not.

Timothy had a sudden insane impulse to walk on past the church hall and into 'The Auld Alliance', the pub on the corner where the High Roads met. No-one had come

10

yet. He wouldn't be seen. Gordon Barber the vice-chairman could take the chair. He'd do it well....Sanity returned and with a feeling of great heaviness in the lower abdomen, Timothy Monteith unlocked the hall door and went inside.

'Gales Week'

Gina Holwell walked briskly down Fairview Avenue. Gina Holwell did everything briskly. Her story is detailed in chapter 7, but it is enough to know at this point that she had undergone a number of experiences in the past few years, culminating in her attendance at a meeting of 'Wholeness for London' where her deep depression had been halted in its tracks and a new sense of the Spirit of God had swept through her.

She was forty-six, had appeared to be fifty-six and now, as some of her acquaintances observed, looked thirty-six.

Some months after the 'Wholeness for London' meeting Gina, with Diana Monteith, Timothy's wife, and Walter and Vivien James went to 'Gales Week'. This was the name popularly given to a large Christian convention held in a holiday camp on the Welsh coast. It wasn't really called 'Gales Week', but the wind always seemed to blow hardest just at that point at that time of the year and those who attended saw it as a fitting sign that the Holy Spirit was present. He was certainly present with the group from St Barnabas'.

All four returned glowing, not only physically (from the combination of wind and sun) but also spiritually from the healing and renewing experiences that had come to them in different ways during the week.

But in addition to their individual experiences had been the influence of other Christians on them as they had talked with them over meals and in long windswept walks on the clifftops.

They had discovered that many churches were being not only renewed in their mode of worship but *rebuilt* to accommodate new forms of activity. Those congregations that could not afford to rebuild their church (or whose ancient buildings were protected from such architectural revolution) were often in the process of moving the furniture about, bringing the Lord's Table down from the east end of the church and placing it in the centre surrounded by chairs in concentric circles; closing off the chancel; abolishing the robed choir; dismissing the organist...

These were heady notions and had been the origin of Item Six on the agenda for the church council, proposing that the pews be removed to allow for 'greater freedom of worship'.

By 'greater freedom' Gina meant room for the music group to expand with a large percussion section and room for worship in dance. Both of these features had caught her attention in 'Gales Week' and she saw them as avenues for the enrichment of St Barnabas' worship.

She crossed the road and paused to call at number 30. Fred Jenkins was a new member of the church council. They could discuss the meeting as they walked together.

Fred Jenkins, in fact, was new to the Christian faith. He had long been an occasional attender at the church, but had been very discouraging to his daughter Carol in her enthusiasm for all things spiritual. Then she had passed her 'A' level exams, which she saw as an answer to prayer. Next Fred had formed a friendship with Gordon Barber, the church treasurer, who had helped him to understand this new dimension.

One evening Fred had attended a home group at which

he had met several members of the Canwell Christian Fellowship, which held exciting services in 'Bingolympia' (formerly the Odeon Cinema) in High Road South. At the meeting Fred had been invited to give his life to the Lord and this he had done. Not only so, but he too had been filled with a new warmth, the gift of tongues and a sense of constant amazement that it could have happened to him. His wife, Joan, did not hide her dismay. His daughter, Carol, did not hide her delight.

And now Fred and Gina walked down the road together and met Walter and Vivien James at the corner of Highwood Avenue. Deep in discussion, the supporters of Item Six advanced towards the church hall, ready for the opposition.

Supporters of tradition

The opposition was not to be dismissed easily. It was spearheaded by church elder Cyril Kent, now seventy-eight, but vigorous and very clear-minded. He was supported by Jane Goodrich, free from her mother for the whole evening, Margaret Barber, Gordon's wife, and Bob Renshaw, a rather eccentric bachelor who lived in a flat in Basingstock Road. The upholders of tradition and orderly worship were a force to be reckoned with. Their motto (from the King James Version of the Bible) was 1 Corinthians 14:40, 'Let all things be done decently and in order.'

By 'decently and in order' they meant 'as they have always been done ever since we can remember'. The services had already been altered by the adoption of the Alternative Service Book. The Bible readings were taken, in Cyril's words 'from any old modern concoction you like'. He failed to see the humour of Gordon's remark that 'old modern' didn't sound quite right.

These changes, together with the falling apart (literally) of Hymns Ancient and Modern, had been accepted grudgingly but fairly quietly, but now, the *pews!* 'They' were threatening to alter the whole nature of the church by destroying the *pews*. The pews had been in place for eighty-five years. They were hard and uncomfortable, certainly, but they stood for security and orderliness. People were arranged in rows, neatly and respectfully. Since they could see only the back of the neck of the person in front there was no embarrassment about being looked at. A pew is a solid item of furniture. One can kneel at it without its shooting forward as a chair does. Books fit on the shelf attached to the pew in front (what *do* you do with your books when everyone sits on *chairs*?).

Anyway the change would cost far more than the church could afford and 'lots' of the older people would leave if the pews were removed. These were the arguments being marshalled by the traditionalists in Cyril Kent's car, as he called for them on the way to the meeting. In fact only one person had threatened to leave and that was Mrs Beesley, but she had threatened to leave many times over many issues, but was still to be found in her place every Sunday, complaining all the time that Canon George would have done it better.

The occupants of Cyril's car arrived at the door of the hall just as the walking party turned into the car park. There were volleys of 'good evenings' and exaggeratedly friendly greetings as they moved together into the hall and sat down on opposite sides of the centre gangway...

Item Six

The atmosphere was brittle, and the opening prayer and preliminary remarks, carefully prepared by Timothy to be delivered in a joyful, carefree voice, came over as tense and nervous. The apologies for absence, the minutes of the last meeting, the matters arising, were all ground out in mechanical fashion like the workings of an old-fashioned mill which inevitably must arrive at Item Six.

Item Four provided some relief, a report by Walter on the Men's Society annual old people's outing. Walter had a wicked sense of the ridiculous and produced a hilarious report, which eased the tension somewhat. But the report lasted for only three minutes.

Item Five was 'Vicar's report'. Few (including Timothy himself) could remember what Timothy reported.

Item Six.

'Let's be honest with one another,' Timothy heard himself saying, 'the next item is one which has aroused great interest and quite a bit of difficulty. We shall all come to it in love and care for one another, wanting to see each other's point of view. I suggest that we pause for prayer before we begin the discussion:

'O Lord, you know our hearts and you know what is best for our church. Thank you for leading us thus far. Guide us in our discussion now so that your will, not ours, shall be done, through Jesus Christ our Lord, Amen.'

Only a few people joined in the 'Amen'. Gina and her party had assumed that 'Your will, not ours, shall be done' meant that the Vicar was on the side of the traditionalists. Cyril and his party had assumed the opposite. Both were sure that God was on their side.

The minutes of the church council meeting of that

evening record the points made for and against and minutes are not interesting to most people. They shall not be repeated here. Emotions were, of course, running high (a factor not recorded in the minutes). Speeches were made like, 'They've already taken our prayer book and our hymn book and brought in coffee and guitars. Where will it end? A tea-urn on the holy table? Cabaret in the pulpit?' and, 'Why should we be held up and prevented from following God's way just because a few old-fashioned people want to kneel on hassocks and remember Queen Victoria? The church is for *young* people, the people of the future.'

Drawing the 'discussion' to a close, Timothy had appealed again for unity, strongly urging both sides to see the other's point of view. He pointed out that the church was placed in Canwell Park, not by nineteenth-century architects, but by God, to stand as a symbol of security and God's changelessness. The services must provide that security and a firm link with the past, the gospel handed down to us. At the same time Christians were called upon to grow, and growth must mean change.

So both changelessness and change were needed. Neither 'side' was wrong. It was a question of seeing the others' point of view and working together. This was a paradox, a question mark with which we all had to live. It was one of many in the life of the Christian. Living with apparent contradictions was what we were called to do.

The plea fell mainly on deaf ears. The meeting broke into excited small groups after the closing prayer, and Timothy walked sadly home, knowing that only the opening skirmishes had been fought.

Think of something about which you disagree strongly with somebody. Is it possible that you might *both* be right? or both *wrong*?

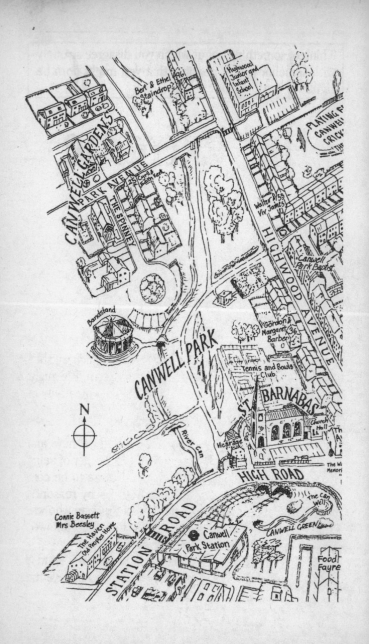

2

The cult of the extreme

These happenings at Canwell Park, to which we shall soon return, are an example of a wider problem. We might call it the cult of the extreme, the 'either/or' mentality of the blinkered mind.

It works like this:

For some reason I suddenly appreciate a new and exciting idea. Let's say that the world is in danger of being over-populated. It doesn't matter how I came to be convinced of this idea, but it is unlikely to be by reasoned argument. Perhaps I admired the wife of the man who was explaining it, or I had had a good day at the office, followed by a good meal and was ready for new ideas.

As soon as this new idea has taken root in my mind it begins to grow. Given exposure to others who believe the same thing, especially if they and/or their wives are attractive or I have good days and good meals, the idea grows very quickly. Its truth becomes more and more obvious to me. Why, it's as plain as a pike-staff. Why doesn't everybody see it? Why don't governments take steps to alleviate the problem before it is too late?

Now while the idea is growing at this pace, everything that seems to oppose it is going to appear in a bad light. Rational arguments are brushed aside. Obvious facts are ignored. A wise and well-informed speaker argues cogently that the world will not become over-populated. I am impatient with his clearly biased views. And I don't think much of his wife either. In any case he's a *Methodist* (read here Anglican, Catholic, Baptist,...anything you are not) so his views can't be sound.

This kind of emotive mixture of half-truths, scarcely-baked arguments and ill-digested facts passes for informed thinking for most of us. Yes, even those of us who read the larger newspapers and pride ourselves on making balanced judgments. We are all inclined to defend our own point of view in a most illogical manner when it is attacked and are very unwilling to accept the fact that our views are held for illogical 'reasons'. And so we tend to extremes. We divide into parties and camps, join societies, give ourselves labels, even wear badges to distinguish ourselves from others with whom we are prepared to disagree. Any day you like.

What hope is there for the human race?

The media push this kind of polarization to the extreme. Two 'experts' are to be interviewed on, shall we say, the problems involved in shutting down an old nuclear power station. One is inclined to favour an expensive but relatively rapid method. The other prefers to leave the reactor to cool down over many years. Both see the other's point of view and are willing to leave the matter as an open question. But the interviewer will have none of that. He is out for entertainment, and that means confrontation, controversy and deadlock. Compromise would be boring. Agreeing to differ would be an admission of defeat for both sides. So stir it up and widen the difference between them as far as possible. He is very skilled in his methods, this interviewer.

Interviewer: 'Sir John. You are on record as saying that it may take a nuclear reactor as much as 500 years to become safe, even after it is closed down. Surely the nation's grandchildren and generations to come cannot tolerate such an appalling prospect.'

Sir John (mildly): 'It all depends what you mean by *safe* you see. The decay of the radio-activity would mean that reasonably safe levels would be reached well before then. I meant that to be totally safe one would have to wait a long time.'

Interviewer (not to be put off so easily): 'But you *implied* that with the reactors we already have, let alone the new ones we might build in the future, this country could become a raging Chernobyl by the year 2050.'

Sir John: 'By no means. I think we can act sensibly now and by spending a few million pounds make safe in a few years what would otherwise take far too long.'

Interviewer (seizing on an opportunity thus offered): 'Sir George what do you say to *that*? A few million pounds. A *few* million pounds. A few *million* pounds. This is just what you are afraid of, isn't it? An escalating drain on the taxpayer's purse running into billions of pounds.'

Sir George (guardedly): 'Well, naturally I would be unwilling to propose any course of action which would waste money, especially the taxpayer's money, but I agree with Sir John...'

Interviewer (hastily interrupting — he can't have these people *agreeing* with one another. It's bad technique): 'Of course, I see that Sir George, but isn't your argument that the short term dismantling of these nuclear stations would be dangerous to the contractors, disastrous to the local inhabitants and prohibitively expensive to the nation?'

Sir George: 'Not really no. I said that I thought it would be better to get the job done steadily rather than rushing too quickly into areas which we don't yet understand.'

Sir John: 'I'm sure you're right there...'

Interviewer: 'And so (and I'm afraid I have to break in there as we're out of time), and so the vicious argument continues. The nuclear industry is split down the middle on a subject which affects our pockets and future generations for up to a thousand years to come. If the experts cannot agree, what hope is there for the human race? Gentlemen, thank you.'

What's going wrong?

So we are inclined by our less than rational habits of behaviour to take sides, to defend our views, to dig ourselves into impregnable positions. And the media reinforce the polarization by making it seem almost wrong to agree with anything or anybody. Abrasiveness is valued. To be accommodating is to be weak and despicable.

Where do the churches stand in all this? Are they beacons of reasonable light in an irrational and dark world? Do Christians see each other's point of view as brothers and sisters and give each other the benefit of the doubt? Do the fellowships of our land brim over with people who agree to differ and delight in their differences?

Gordon and Margaret Barber were walking home after the church council meeting. They said their last goodnight to a small group crossing the road by the war memorial and walked for a short time in silence. Margaret spoke first,

'Gordon.'

'M'm.'

'Do you remember Timothy telling us about Shelley talking to him after church one day and how she thought Barnabas had waved at us all from the stained-glass window? She said, "It's nice here" or something like that. That was less than a year ago. It seems like a hundred. What's going wrong, Gordon?'

'It's difficult to say,' said Gordon thoughtfully. 'All that emphasis on Barnabas and encouragement was really good you know and it still is. Then Gina and her big experience...and Fred, look at the change in Fred.'

'But it's people like Gina and Fred that cause all this trouble. They can't leave things alone. They insist on changing everything. And the old guard can't cope.'

'It isn't only the old guard,' chuckled Gordon. 'You're not *so* old you know.'

'Well, I suppose I do take their side,' said Margaret. 'I suppose I'm a bit conservative too. There's so much change in the world today it's nice to think that at least at church you can find some continuity.'

Their walk up Highwood Avenue was a short one and the conversation was interrupted by their arrival at number 36. Carol Jenkins had been baby-sitting and Fred, her father, had already called on his way home to take her with him. Carol was putting away Margaret's ironing board

23

when they arrived ('Oh Carol you *shouldn't* — I'm sure you have lots of studying to do') and Fred was in full flight, telling her exactly what everyone had said at the meeting. He paused briefly while Margaret and Gordon thanked Carol for the third time and money changed hands, then he was off again. They could hear him as he walked up the avenue, explaining what Cyril had said when Gina had suggested that they should...

Gordon closed the door quietly, but obviously the noise had been too much already because he became aware of a small white-clad figure standing at the bottom of the stairs.

'Shelley pet, aren't you asleep?'

'I could hear you all talking and you woke me up, tho I came to thee what wath happening.'

The blundering buffoon

Shelley was seven. Just. And Shelley had lost her front teeth. This loss was a great problem for her because she hated the undisciplined way her tongue seemed to slip out of gear with no front teeth to contain it. She was very glad to be growing up and proud of her accomplishment in getting rid of her old teeth, but the new ones came, oh so slowly.

'There's nothing for you to worry about, darling. It's silly people at church, arguing with one another because some want things to stay exactly as they are and some want things to change.'

'If they all liked each other more they wouldn't quarrel.'

'I think you're right, pet, but people can't want what *they* want and also want the opposite. But all this is too muddling for you at this time of night. Come on, back to bed!'

But Shelley stood solemnly still and said,

'They can. Simon Peter did. We had him on Sunday.'
She folded her hands in front of her and recited in a sing-song voice:

'He was a brave coward, a weak strong-man, a blundering buffoon and a man of God.'

'Shelley, do you know what a "blundering buffoon" is?'

'No, but it sounds lovely. Blundering buffoon, blundering...'

'To *bed*', said Gordon, taking up his daughter, now helpless with mirth. 'Blundering buffoon indeed.'

Ten minutes later, over a final cup of coffee, Margaret and Gordon were still talking, but very quietly in case Shelley got involved again.

'How *does* that child remember things?' said Gordon. 'I keep telling Gina that seven and eight year olds can't understand all these complicated Bible studies she does, and now my own daughter proves me wrong.'

'Perhaps she doesn't understand things, she just remembers words. Like "blundering buffoon".'

'But she gets them right and uses them in the right context. I think she understood exactly what the problem is you know and I think she may be pointing us to an answer, even if she doesn't realize it. Perhaps it's time we gave Barnabas a rest and had a closer look at Thimon Peter.'

'Gordon, you promised you wouldn't take the mickey. Poor child. Anyway. It's time for sleep not Simon Peter now. But perhaps there's something in what you say...'

And perhaps there was.

Simon Peter

Peter needs no introduction. He is one of the small handful

of Bible names that most people still remember. But what about that name? 'Peter', 'stone' or 'rock'. Jesus gave Simon that name (Matthew 16:18) at a time in his life when he was anything but rock-like. In fact 'blundering buffoon' isn't a bad description of Peter.

He was a fisherman of course, a practical man of action, always ready to jump in (literally at times — John 21:7) where others hung back, thinking about things. A brief look at his letters shows that he was no mean thinker himself, but it seemed that he usually acted first and thought afterwards. He gives the impression of being a large, muscular, open-faced man, no doubt tanned by the sun and wind, immediately approachable, lovable, but perhaps of uncertain temper.

Peter was a man of firm convictions, a loyal and stout-hearted disciple, who cheerfully gave up his life as a fisherman to become a fisher of men (Mark 1:17). He was capable of great faith and great folly. He was a leader among the disciples, yet he denied his Lord. When Jesus revealed his reason for coming to the world, to die for mankind, it was Peter who advised him not to. When Jesus was transfigured and spoke to Moses and Elijah on the mountainside it was Peter who suggested a little memorial building ('he didn't know what he was talking about'). Peter, the most well-meaning of men who frequently opened his mouth and almost as frequently put his foot in it. The Charlie Brown of the New Testament — a round-headed kid with a heart of gold and a talent for disasters. Good grief!

Yet precisely because of all this, Simon Peter is a key to the problem facing the church at Canwell Park and that faces many churches and individuals — how can we live with apparent contradictions? How can we understand the 'both/and' situations we seem to get into? Is it possible to hold two ideas at once, which seem to cancel each other out? And if it is, is it ever *right*? And how can I see the other person's point of view when he/she is so obviously *wrong*?

Simon Peter threads his way through all four gospels and the first part of the book of Acts, and his two letters appear near the end of the New Testament. The Bible without Peter would be a very different book. Perhaps it *is* possible to live with contradictions and survive.

Does this idea of opposites both being true upset you?
Does it confuse you?
Or is it exciting?

3

The swing of the pendulum

The church as a haven of security: the church as a vehicle of change. Not many people in Canwell Park could appreciate that these ideas could be true both at once. And those who could were unwilling to face the consequences.

It's easy to ride the pendulum. We can sit as far out as we like and be extremists. We are exactly opposed to the people who insist on sitting at the other end of the swing.

Another, perhaps more usual, way of riding the pendulum is to swing with it. One day we are convinced by a clear argument in favour of x but the next day we hear an even clearer argument in favour of y. So we swing from one side to the other, bewildering ourselves and anyone who tries to talk to us. It is good to be open to new truths and new interpretations but not if it means dizzying changes of view every other day on matters of importance.

The cautious among us approach the problem more cannily. Because constant, violent swinging from one opinion to its opposite is so uncomfortable, why not compromise? Take half of one and half of the other and stay securely poised in the middle. This sounds fine in theory but some truths refuse to be cut in half. Can you have 50% free will and 50% predestination for instance? The problem becomes ridiculous, like that of Strephon in act one of Gilbert and Sullivan's *Iolanthe* who was half a mortal and half a fairy. He was a fairy down to the waist — but his legs were mortal. As Strephon complained...

What's the use of being half a fairy? My body can creep through a keyhole, but what's the good of that when my legs are left kicking behind?...my upper half is immortal, but my lower half grows older every day, and some day or other must die of old age. What's to become of my upper half when I've buried my lower half I really don't know.

Besides, if you stop the pendulum in the middle, the clock won't go.

Then finally, is there a possibility that we should be at both ends of the pendulum swing at once? But that's impossible. Perhaps it isn't. It's just the way some things work.

Consider for instance the questions, should I love myself? and am I worth anything? Yes or no?

Am I worth anything?

Cyril and Edith Kent were deep in discussion, their faces bathed in light. The light was reflected from the frozen food dispenser in the Food Fayre supermarket and their discussion centred on the relative merits of chump chops or mini-steaks for Sunday lunch. As usual on Saturday morning elbow room was scarce so they hardly noticed when Gina Holwell's trolley collided with theirs. Too late to change course, Gina had to greet them.

'Gina, dear,' said Mrs Kent, leaving her husband to make the crucial decision about the Sunday lunch, 'how *are* you? I hear you had a busy time at the church council meeting last week. It's all very exciting isn't it!'

Gina smiled warily and Cyril grunted, and chose chops.

'Actually, I'm glad to see you,' said Gina, almost truthfully, 'I wanted to apologize to you Cyril for being rather outspoken in the meeting, especially as you're an elder in the church. I wasn't very tactful I'm afraid.'

'Don't worry about that,' said Cyril, suddenly warming, as he often did, into an unexpected smile. 'We were all rather heated I think. In any case, you have no need to apologize to me. I'm not worth apologizing to.'

'*Cyril!*' said Edith.

'Of *course* you're worth apologizing to,' said Gina, taken aback. 'Everyone is. And you're especially important to the church as an elder and to God as one of his children — oh there I go preaching again.'

'No', said Cyril firmly, 'I accept your apology of course in the spirit in which it was meant but I am really not worthy of it. "I am but a worm and no man." The Scripture is quite clear on that point. John the Baptist was right when he said, "He (that is Jesus) must increase and I must decrease." My aim is to stand out of the way and let Christ be all in all.'

'I wish you would stand out of the way and let me get to the frozen food.'

The voice sounded harsh, but the speaker was Gordon Barber, doing a poor imitation of an old lady.

'Gordon, I am sorry, yes of course.' Cyril was covered with confusion as he made way for Gordon, Margaret and Shelley.

'So *Gordon* is worth apologizing to,' pursued Gina.

'I don't apologize because of his worth, but because I was in his way,' said Cyril. 'Gordon's a good Christian' ('Thanks very much,' muttered Gordon, but not loud enough to be heard) 'and he too is a channel. "Channels only, blessed master." Don't you remember what the apostle Paul said to the Philippians in chapter three verse eight: "Yea doubtless," (he always used the King James Version of the Bible) "and I count all things but loss for the excellency of the knowledge of Christ Jesus my Lord: for whom I have suffered the loss of all things, and do count them but dung, that I may win Christ." He must be everything. I must be nothing, nothing.'

As he often did, Cyril had become absorbed in his theme and his voice had become louder and louder. When he pronounced the word 'dung', Shelley Barber screamed with delight and jumped up and down.

'He said dung Mummy.'

'Yes dear, hush.'

A few moments later the store manager interrupted to break up the knot of shoppers which had gathered and was blocking the gangway. As she moved on, Gina was heard to remark partly to herself and partly to Gordon, ' "Oh to be nothing, nothing." It may be good

Buddhism, but it's bad Christianity.'

'Thank you Father for making me me.'

Fifteen minutes later, the Barber family crossed High Road South and made their way to the row of shops called, rather grandly, 'The Mall'. There, on the pavement, they encountered what appeared at first to be a small open-air revivalist meeting, but what was in fact an excited group of teenage girls, Carol Jenkins, Rachel Hughes and Sharon Zoltanowski, with Carol's dad, Fred, and mum, Joan. All five were speaking at once but when the Barbers appeared they were hailed with delight and drawn into the group.

'We were just saying, Gordon, how good it is to know that you're really *somebody* when you're a Christian,' said Fred. 'It's wonderful to have assurance that you matter. You can be yourself without apologizing.'

'Yes, but...' said Margaret.

'You've always got a "but",' said Fred. 'What's this but?'

'Well there is a danger of being self-centred and over-doing the self-love business. Surely we should love other people and think more of them than our own importance.'

'That's what I keep telling him.' Joan made an attempt to find a gap in which to say something, and found one. 'He's always going on these days about, "I'm OK, you're OK" or something, and you've got to love yourself before you can love other people. Gordon. You won't let me down now. What do you think about it?'

Gordon opened his mouth to give his usual careful and balanced answer when his opinion was sought but the three girls got there first and burst into song:

You gave me a heart and you gave me a smile,

32

You gave me Jesus and you made me your child
And I just thank you Father for making me me.

'That's the butterfly song,' said Shelley. 'I love that one.'
Shopping was not quite as boring as she had expected.

Gordon opened his mouth again, but this time Margaret
spoke first.

'That's just it. "You gave me Jesus." It sounds as if the
whole universe was created just for your personal benefit.
That song makes *me* the centre of everything.'

'It is a children's song,' said Gordon mildly.

'But you *are* at the centre of everything,' said Carol, 'and
so am I. Dad's right you know.'

'Well I think,' said Gordon firmly, 'I think you're both
right and if we don't finish the shopping soon, Shelley will
miss her ballet class.'

'They can't both be right'

'The universe is so enormous.'

Shelley was safely at her ballet class and Gordon and
Margaret were thankfully quiet again with coffee in the
kitchen. Margaret had broken the silence.

'Why do you say that?'

'Well, how can I, or you, or Fred, be so important? We're
like little specks of dust on the earth and the earth is like
a little speck of dust in the solar system, and the solar
system is like...I mean you can go on and on. And God
must be bigger than all of it because he made it. How can
such an infinitely small speck be important, except to itself
and the speck or two next to it?'

'It isn't just a question of size is it?' said Gordon, reaching
for a biscuit.

'No, of course not,' snorted Margaret, 'I'm not as naive as all that. But. Well, I can understand that God can concentrate on several billion things and people at once — I don't know *how* but I can believe that he does. But if you have to share his love with billions of other people, it does *dilute* it a bit. I suppose I feel a bit jealous of all the others, if I'm honest.'

'I think it all goes back to John 3:16, doesn't it?' said Gordon, 'God loved the world so much that it was worth giving his only Son, and so on.'

'Yes, but there it is again, he loved "the world". That's all of us. Collectively. Like a herd.'

'Of course it is,' said Gordon, 'God's not going to love *you* and forget about the rest of us! But seriously, don't you remember Tim's sermon when he said that God has enough love for an infinite number of people and enough love so that if I were the only sinner on earth, Jesus would still have died just for me. That butterfly song you so much dislike is right you know. How can I judge how valuable I am? Not by comparing myself with other people, but by asking, What price tag does God put on me? I am important enough for God to have created me; important enough for God, in Christ his Son, to die for me; important enough for God, in his Spirit, to live in me and develop my potential. That's what Tim said, I think. It's amazing!'

'I suppose it is,' said Margaret doubtfully, 'But are you joining the "love yourself" brigade? You know, "I did it *my* way".'

'Not if "love yourself" means "me first", "self-fulfilment is everything" and "down with the rest", no. But if it means that I understand how valuable I am in God's sight, then yes, I think so. It's a basis for worship and a *proper* basis for loving others...What's the matter?'

34

Gordon broke off suddenly as he saw a look of horror spread over his wife's face. Was all this new truth too much for her? Was theological discussion not a good idea on a Saturday morning?

'Gordon, it's half-past twelve!'

'Good grief!'

Gordon was out of his chair in a moment and scrambling for his car like a Battle-of-Britain fighter pilot.

'Old Ma Higgs'll shoot me.'

'Old Ma Higgs', who preferred to be known as 'Madame Narina', ran the ballet class, which concluded *promptly* at 12.30. Madame Narina did not enjoy waiting for parents who came late to collect their offspring. The theological discussion ended abruptly.

Do you love yourself? Why/why not?
How can a Christian use his/her gifts fully without falling into the temptation of pride and demanding self-fulfilment?
Psalm 8 describes our worth in God's estimation. Have a look at it.

4
Real reality

We are in danger of getting confused. Perhaps it's time to stand back and ask a few basic questions before accompanying Simon Peter in a slice of real reality.

We'll join the congregation of St Barnabas', Canwell Park, as Timothy Monteith, vicar, pastor, counsellor and friend to his flock, gets underway with his Sunday morning sermon. Everyone is sitting in a posture of rapt attention. All eyes are on the preacher. Some minds are too. He warms to his subject:

It is fascinating to see how people's minds work, isn't it? There are some people here who will believe something only when they've fully understood it, thrashed it all out and got it fair and square in their minds. Then there are

*others who despair of understanding ideas at all, especially
ideas about faith. They say, 'It's all too much for me. I'll
leave the difficult stuff to the Vicar. Don't bother me with
doctrine. My mind is too ordinary for that.'*

*In a sense both people have a good point. Yes, we've
been given minds to use and we ought to use them to the
very limit of their capacity (yes, there is no excuse for being
lazy!) but, on the other hand, our minds are limited and
we cannot expect to be able to understand all that there
is to know about God. We need a lot of humility. So where
do we draw the line?*

*Let's take the example of this 'both/and' business. We
were thinking about it last week. You won't believe this,
but I'll tell you anyway. Only two people talked to me
about the sermon last week. One said, 'I do like the idea
of opposite things both being true. It made me realize that
life really is like that, if I'm humble enough to recognize
it.' The other said, 'I don't agree at all about opposite things
being true. To begin with, they can't be, and secondly,
you could believe anything — black is white, good is evil,
God is the devil...where would it end?'*

Well, where will it end?

*To help us answer this question, I'd like to refer to this
little book, published some years ago. It's by J. I. Packer
and it's called* Evangelism and the Sovereignty of God.
*At one point he deals with these 'both/ands', the baffling
riddles which seem to have no answer. He says that they
come in two different forms and it is very important to
decide which is which.*

At this point, Carol Jenkins' eyes became glazed, Mrs
Beesley's head slumped forward and Jane Goodrich sat
up straighter.

The first is called paradox. 'God's service is perfect freedom.' How can slavery and freedom fit together? The church's unchanging tradition is to encourage growth and variety. How can it be unchanging if it grows? The paradox is a word puzzle. Something is stated in a puzzling way, perhaps to attract attention. 'Dying, we live,' cries St Paul.

But the puzzle can be explained. Work it out and all becomes clear. A paradox is only an apparent contradiction. Provide the key and the problem is unlocked.

God's service is perfect freedom because we are created to be at our best as we relate humbly to him and are freed from sin and selfishness. A fish finds true freedom to be itself only when it is imprisoned (!) in water.

The church preserves tradition at its best when it passes down to each generation the need for new life, growth and a variety of gifts.

Paul's spiritual life depended on his 'dying' to selfishness and pride and being alive to God.

So much of what we see as contradiction is only apparently so. It's paradoxical because it is stated as if it were a contradiction. A few words of explanation unravel the tangle.

But there's another kind of contradiction which does not depend on the way it's expressed. There really is a conflict and however clever you are you will never explain it. Scientists talk about light as consisting of particles and also as behaving like waves. Take my word for it that light can be accurately described in both ways and they do not fit together — they exclude one another. Yet, they're both true. So what do you do? You have to grin and bear it. No amount of algebra will explain that one.

Packer calls this an antinomy, but it's easier to use the word mystery. The obvious example from the Bible is predestination and free will. If God knows all about us and all about the world (and if he doesn't he's not God) he knows what we will do next. This means that we have no choice and the Bible makes it clear that we do. God told Moses, for instance, that the choice of life and death was before Israel. 'Now choose life' (Deuteronomy 30:19).

Both predestination and free will exist, yet they cannot be understood together. There is no key that will explain the contradiction — they are apparently mutually exclusive. So we must resign ourselves to calling this a mystery, something which our minds cannot wrap themselves around, and, as Packer says, 'learn to live with it'.

God's mind can understand even these mysteries.

Now beware! Some people have used this idea of mysteries as an excuse for not believing facts which the Bible assumes to be real. The resurrection of Jesus is a good example. It's a mystery. Well, yes it is. But it's not one of those 'both/and' mysteries so that it did happen and did not happen both at the same time.

The Bible, and Christian tradition based on the Bible, make it quite clear that the bodily resurrection did take place and, whether modern man chooses to believe it or not, it was a fact, an occurrence which really happened. Christianity has always been based on the belief that certain things are absolutely true; that God is and that he can be found if you really look for him (Hebrews 11:6), that Jesus really lived, really died for our sins and really rose from the grave. These basic facts are recited weekly by many of us in our creed, our public confession of belief.

Christians stand foursquare against the idea that truth doesn't matter, that any idea is as good as any other.

But wait a minute...

Earlier on we were saying that there are mysteries, truths

which appear to be self-contradictory, which our minds will never understand. Now we're claiming that Christianity is based on certain facts and that truth is not negotiable. We're open to the charge of wandering in circles.

The obvious answer to that one is that some truths are absolute and not negotiable and do not have an equal and opposite aspect. Others do. Some are genuine mysteries. Some are just paradoxical statements. The challenge to us is to work out which is which. Our guide book is the Bible. Our guide is the Holy Spirit. It's not just a discussion question for philosophers. It matters in everyday life. May the Lord give us wisdom in discerning the one from the other.

The service over, opinions about the sermon begin to flow:

'Dry as dust today. Sounded like he'd swallowed a theology textbook.' This was Carol Jenkins.

'Not sufficiently biblical. Too abstract.' Cyril Kent.

'Didn't understand a word 'e was on about.' Mrs Beesley.

'Very good foundation for our working together.' Gordon Barber.

'I do love the way he pushes the hair out of his eyes.' Rachel Hughes.

'Thanks, Timothy.' Jane Goodrich.

Reality revealed

It was a very long, hot and exhausting climb. Once again Jesus had acted mysteriously, inviting his three closest followers to come away with him on an unknown errand. There had been speculation on the lower slopes as to whether there would be another four, five, or even ten thousand to feed. How long would they be away? Mount Hermon was nearly 3,000 metres high. Were they going to the top? Or was this to be a quiet retreat for the four of them in some shaded valley on the hillside?

Jesus was uncommunicative and seemed to be full of his own thoughts. As the day wore on and the heat increased, the questions died away and the grim realities of thirst and heat and weariness claimed all their attention.

At last Jesus halted and they sank exhausted; Peter, James and John, tough fishermen but not mountaineers, were almost immediately asleep.

Peter was the first to awake. In that troubled half-conscious moment between sleep and wakefulness, especially when one is uncomfortable and hot, he thought he was looking straight at the sun. He turned away, dazzled, and was astonished to see the sun, sinking now in the west. What then was this brilliant light? Shielding his eyes he looked again and saw an amazing and totally unexpected sight: Jesus, his face and clothing actually shining and, reflected in the light of his radiance, two other men, talking to him.

James and John were struck dumb when they saw the group, but Peter was on his feet in an instant.

'Master, what a privilege it is for us to be here. We must make a permanent memorial to this wonderful meeting. Let's build three shrines, one for each of you. Jesus, Moses, Elijah...'

He became incoherent. He didn't know what to say next. How had he guessed who these people were? Surely he'd said all the wrong things. How had he dared to speak at all? While he was still blundering on, a cloud appeared and enveloped them all. Their terror increased when they

41

heard a voice, apparently in the cloud, saying, 'This is my Son, whom I have chosen; listen to him.'

The cloud evaporated. The sun returned. Jesus was alone. What had all this meant? Jesus had shown them a slice of real reality. For a while they had seen him as he really was, heard who he was and sensed the awe of the majesty of God. The veil had been lifted, the lid removed. Absolute light and power and love had been shown to them. Reality. But, as T. S. Eliot wrote in *Four Quartets*, 'Humankind cannot bear very much reality'. Instead of worshipping and taking in the wonder of it all, Peter had to respond by reducing reality to his own framework ('set up a plaque here to commemorate the occasion').

Reality is there if we will see it. It is *here* if we will accept it. But, like Peter, we are not accustomed to the brightness of the light and we turn to something more familiar and comfortable. George Eliot expressed this idea in *Middlemarch*:

> *If we had a keen vision and feeling of all ordinary human life, it would be like hearing the grass grow and the squirrel's heart beat, and we should die of that roar which lies on the other side of silence. As it is, the quickest of us walk about well wadded with stupidity.*

But we should not die if we opened ourselves to the real presence of God. Perhaps that is what he wants us to do but we see only a confused picture of God, not the reality at all.

Distorting mirrors

We live, as it were, in a small room containing a distorting mirror, a window, open to the night sky, and a bright light. We look for God. We look for God where it seems comfortable to look; in the mirror. What we see is, of course, a distorted reflection of ourselves. The happy person sees a positive God; the depressed person sees a judgmental God.

But we are unwilling to switch off the light and let our eyes get accustomed to the starlight where the real God can be viewed in his timeless and awe-inspiring majesty. Our God is not only too small — we look for him in the wrong places and see only a reflection of ourselves. Peter's God was too small. He thought in terms of memorials instead of majesty, of plaques instead of paradise.

'I think,' said Margaret Barber, as the family walked home after the service, 'that Tim has helped us, you know. It's quite a new challenge to decide what is paradox and what is mystery — to know the limits of our being able to explain things.'

'And I think,' said Gordon her husband, 'that he was very helpful in showing us that there is real reality behind all the appearances of things. We need to be able to look in the right place for it.'

'And *I* think,' said Shelley, who hadn't heard the sermon, but had been in the Climbers' Group, '*I* think that all that is very muddly. I think that we should think about *Jesus* just like Auntie Gina said.'

'And I think,' said Gordon, 'that you're right, Shelley. He is paradox and mystery and clear, plain reality as well, and in him we really know where we are.'

After reading this chapter (if you have!) are you inclined
to want to stop thinking about such problems?
Or are you encouraged to push on to the frontier of
your thinking capacity?
Can you see where Jesus fits into it all?

5

Voices and pictures

Cicely Staindrop sighed deeply, placed her Bible on the side-table next to her wheelchair and looked at her husband over her glasses.

'What *is* the matter with you, Bert?' she said. 'You can't keep still for two minutes together. Is it all about Catharine?'

Catharine had been Bert's elder sister. She had died a month ago at the age of eighty-five.

'Yes it is actually. Surely there's something we can do about Catharine.'

'You can't *do* anything,' said his wife gently. 'She's beyond our help now. We must trust the good Lord to look after her and leave her in his hands.'

'Well I'm not so sure that there isn't something we can

45

do when all's said and done.'

'Like what for instance?'

'Like, well, like making contact. It happens quite a lot, you know. Making contact.' Bert spoke half wistfully, half apologetically.

'Do you mean magic? because I'm not having anything to do with that.' Mrs Staindrop was emphatic.

'No, no, no. It's not *magic*. It's very spiritual. They sing hymns. It's like another church really. But instead of just talking and singing about heaven they get down to real business and contact people there. They hear their voices.'

'Bert Staindrop. I do not understand you,' said his wife, raising both hands and letting them fall again in a gesture of helplessness. 'All these years you've taken me to church and brought me home afterwards. Not once have you agreed to come inside, not *once*. And now you're asking me to believe that the spiritualists can be more use than a straightforward Christian church. What's got into you, Bert? It don't seem right.'

'It's like I said,' Bert was warming to his subject, 'Allan and Marge have this little meeting up the road. It's in their house. You don't go into a temple or anything. They turn the lights down and really get in touch with their relations or friends. It would be wonderful to know that Catharine is at peace you know, Cicely. Wonderful.'

Much against her better judgment and because Bert was so distressed at the loss of his sister (although they had hardly met for the previous twenty years) and because she had the idea that any interest in matters spiritual was better than none, she reluctantly agreed to go to the next séance at 'Allan and Marge's up the road'.

Voices

As Bert had promised, the atmosphere was warm and welcoming. Bert and his wife were introduced to the gathering, about ten strong, and Mrs Staindrop's defences began to weaken.

Mrs Porter was introduced. Mrs Porter was a medium. She was middle-aged and wore her hair short-cropped and seemed a very matter-of-fact person, Mrs Staindrop thought, a bit like Gina Holwell. Not a bit like a witch or anything of that sort. Her eyes didn't seem sinister even.

The lights were turned down so that the faces of everyone in the circle became indistinct.

'Now has anyone a loved one they want to contact?' Mrs Porter was saying. 'Someone we need a word from maybe.'

Someone mentioned his mother who had, as he put it, 'passed over' some months ago but he was sure that she was not at peace. He had a feeling that she was about the house all the time and it was a worry to him.

Eyes were closed and there was a long silence. Mrs Porter began to make noises in her throat, somewhere between a snore and a cough. At length she spoke in a deep, unnatural-sounding voice at which the young man became very tense and excited and called out, 'Mother, mother, is that you?'

He was assured that it really was his mother, that she was not at all distressed and that she promised not to make her son feel uneasy about her any more.

Mrs Porter seemed to be quite exhausted after this and there was a pause.

Then Bert took the opportunity to ask whether Catharine might be contacted.

'Catharine is your sister?' He noticed that Mrs Porter

didn't say 'was your sister'. How did she know that about the relationship anyway?

The voice this time was much higher pitched. Catharine had had a high-pitched voice, even in old age. She seemed to be assuring Bert that she was fine and he needn't worry about her.

Mrs Staindrop broke in: 'Where are you Catharine?'

'Over here. In a better place,' came the answer.

'Who is with you?'

'We're all here. I'm not lonely.'

'Is Jesus there?'

A pause, then, 'Yes, of course Jesus is here. We're all here.'

'Is Jesus Christ the Lord, our Saviour there in glory?' persisted Mrs Staindrop.

'This is quite unnecessary and distressing,' said Mrs Porter suddenly. 'Please turn up the lights. If you are unable to co-operate then we cannot continue with this meeting.'

'One other question,' said Mrs Staindrop, who had obviously been doing some research, 'Are you a member of the National Spiritualists Union?'

'Well, no,' said Mrs Porter, 'but that's not necessary.'

Mrs Staindrop said she was sorry but perhaps it was time to go.

When they got home, Bert was predictably annoyed. 'What did you have to go and do that for?' he said. 'We were getting on really well. Catharine's all right. You heard her. Then you had to go and spoil it.'

'Catharine's all right maybe. But did we hear *her*?'

'It was her voice. It was real.'

'Was it?' said Mrs Staindrop.

Pictures

At the time that the séance was taking place in Highwood Avenue, Diana Monteith was leading an informal meeting of prayer and praise in the vicarage. The three teenagers, Carol, Rachel and Sharon were there as was Gina Holwell, Fred Jenkins and Walter and Viv James.

They sat in an informal circle, drank some coffee and sang some worship songs. Then came the time for prayer.

'I feel that the Lord is very specially close to us this evening,' Diana was saying, 'and that he wants to speak to us, to say something that we need to know. If anyone sees a picture while we're praying do be ready to share it with us all afterwards and we'll try to discern, with the Spirit's help, what he is saying to us. Or perhaps a word of prophecy will be given, or a particular word from Scripture.'

A thrill of excitement passed through the group. Jesus was present with them, by his Spirit, and they could not only speak to him but receive messages from him.

They prayed. They listened. They worshipped.

After the prayer they shared the pictures that had come to them and were astonished that they made good sense when they compared them. Carol had seen, in her mind's eye, a great cathedral, full of people. Fred contributed a fountain, flowing with clear water. Gina saw a road, fringed with trees, lit by the sun.

It was clear that they were being shown that their church was to be led along the right way, under the warm light of God's grace. It would be cleansed in the stream of the clear water of the spring of God's goodness and become a great church, full of worshipping people. It was very heartwarming, a very real experience.

What's going on?

Two meetings, taking place on the same evening, in the same suburb, not half a mile apart. How do they compare? Voices or pictures? What's going on here? Is this just another case of 'both/and', both equally valid experiences, both right? Or is this a situation where if one is true and valid the other is not? What was Timothy's formula? 'Our guide book is the Bible. Our guide is the Holy Spirit.'

So how does the Bible guide us to evaluate these gatherings? There can be little doubt that communication with the dead is not what God wants, if we take the Bible seriously.

The episode of King Saul, requesting the medium of Endor to call up the spirit of Samuel, described in 1 Samuel 28, makes it clear that such communication is not only wrong but, in Saul's case at least, a prologue to death.

In the New Testament, Jesus had little to say directly on the subject, but let fall a telling phrase as he told the story of the rich man and Lazarus: '...between us and you a great chasm has been fixed, so that those who want to go from here to you cannot, nor can anyone cross over from there to us' (Luke 16:26). Heaven and hell are here intended, but it seems likely that communication between heaven (or hell) and earth is also forbidden by a 'great gulf'.

There is nothing in the whole Bible which encourages us to communicate with the dead. Mediums are forbidden in the Old Testament (*e.g.* Deuteronomy 18:10–12, 'Let no-one be found among you who...is a medium or spiritist or who consults the dead. Anyone who does these things is detestable to the Lord') and silenced in the New (see Acts 16:16–18). It looks as if the meeting at Allan and Marge's, however well-intentioned, could not claim to be Christian, nor to conform to biblical ideals. And why did Mrs Staindrop's insistence on asking about Jesus Christ the Lord cause such embarrassment?

The voice they heard was not the voice of Catharine.

It might still be argued that the meeting at Allan and Marge's was just a bit of harmless fun. Even if some trickery was going on it was doing no damage. But this kind of involvement with the unknown is not necessarily trickery. Not human trickery, anyhow. There is a very unpleasant reality lurking behind the apparently 'spiritual' exterior and many people have been spiritually confused and even oppressed by evil as a result of their involvement. This is not an option for the Christian believer.

What about the prayer meeting then? God certainly calls his people to pray. Jesus promised that when two or three meet in his name he would be present (Matthew 18:20). But these pictures. Are they any different from the voices heard in Highwood Avenue?

There is no specific instruction in Old or New Testaments that we are to expect pictures in our minds or otherwise, though Joel predicted that the old should dream dreams and the young see visions before the great day of the Lord (Joel 2:28). But there is much in the Bible about God speaking to his people and guiding them, and much in the New Testament about the gifts of the Spirit which include 'the message of wisdom', ' the message of knowledge', 'prophecy' and so on (see 1 Corinthians 12:4–11). There seems no reason why God should not choose to communicate visually, through dreams or through imaginative prayer. He made himself known visually very often. For example, the Lord called to Ananias 'in a vision' (Acts 9:10).

But are the recipients of these pictures seeing them clearly? Are they interpreting them correctly? Are they just

51

making them up? These are all dangers which need to be honestly faced. This is no party game where the players close their eyes, think of the first thing that comes into their heads and assume it to be the will of God!

This kind of prayer needs to be humbly and carefully approached. A group needs to be led by a mature person. Members need to be ready to admit that they may be mistaken. No picture that is contrary to the clear teaching of the Bible may be entertained. The second of Timothy's two guide-lines must be involved, 'Our guide is the Holy Spirit.'

So Christians at prayer may be mistaken about the guidance they receive but they are in no doubt that the guidance does come from God himself because he promised that those who ask will receive, those who seek will find and those who knock will have the door opened for them (Matthew 7:7).

It begins to look as if the séance was looking in the wrong direction for guidance while the prayer meeting was facing the right way. Both were sincere. But they were looking in diametrically opposed directions. The *source* of the illumination matters. The source is not within ourselves but outside.

Simon Peter provides us with a dramatic illustration of this fact.

Have you ever tried to contact a departed person?
Have you ever seriously tried to contact God?
If contacting the dead is wrong, what was Jesus doing with Moses and Elijah?

6

'You are the Messiah'

About a week before the transfiguration described in chapter 4 (to be precise the gospels vary between six and eight days in their reports of the occasion), Jesus and his disciples were enjoying one of their periods of peace and quiet, away from the crowds. They were near Caesarea Philippi, to the north of the Sea of Galilee, an upland area of great beauty. The incidents are described in three of the gospels (Matthew 16:13–23, Mark 8:27–33 and Luke 9:18–22). The details vary. In Mark the Lord and his disciples are on the way to Caesarea; in Luke they are praying together in private. But the important central theme is the same in all three accounts.

Suddenly, Jesus asked them a question:

'Who do the crowds say that I am? What do they make

of me, do you think?'

There followed a chorus of replies. The people who had heard Jesus had a variety of theories as to who he was.

John the Baptist, returned from the dead, was a popular notion. There was some substance in the idea: both had preached a call to repentance. There may have been a family likeness (their mothers had been cousins). But the enthusiasts for this view forgot a rather obvious fact: Jesus and John were contemporaries. They had known each other. If Jesus had suddenly become John the Baptist now, who had he been before? Ridiculous!

Some said he was Elijah. A well-established Jewish belief (based on Malachi 4:5) claimed that Elijah would return as a forerunner of the Messiah. Indeed part of the Passover celebrations includes to this day the pouring of wine for Elijah and sometimes sending children to the door to see whether he has come yet. Elijah seemed a likely candidate to some.

How about Jeremiah, back in human form? If we once open the door to reincarnated prophets the list is a long one.

Jesus allowed the disciples to discuss cheerfully what the current ideas were. Then, without warning, he cut across their discussion:

'But what about you? Who do *you* say I am?'

There was an awkward silence. It was one thing to discuss the latest rumours from the marketplace, to throw back and forth the theories of other people. But to be asked point-blank, 'What do *you* think?' was different. If they said, 'A carpenter from Nazareth', they would be dodging the issue. If they said, 'A prophet', they would be merely joining the crowds in the marketplace. If they said 'God', they would be uttering a blasphemy and one that perhaps

54

most of them were not prepared to commit themselves to. No wonder there was a pause.

Peter broke the silence with a typically rash statement: 'You are the Messiah, the Son of the Living God.'

The disciples were aghast. What had Peter said? Did he realize, dear old blundering Peter, that he was more or less claiming that their friend was God? Surely Jesus would round on him and put him firmly in his place — 'How dare you suggest such a thing!'

But Jesus turned to Peter with warmth and gratitude, and to the utter astonishment of the others, said:

'Blessed are you, Simon, son of Jonah, for this was not revealed to you by man, but by my Father in heaven. And I tell you that you are Peter, and on this rock I will build my church, and the gates of Hades will not overcome it' (Matthew 16:17–18).

The significant point here is that Peter had been open to an outside source for his statement. It wasn't an idea he had made up. He had spoken an inspired message that came from God himself.

'Out of my sight, Satan!'

What happened next is therefore the more astonishing.

Jesus began to explain to his followers that, as Christ or Messiah, Son of God, he must suffer greatly at the hands of the 'church' leaders of the day, that he must be killed and that he would come back to life on the third day from his death.

Of course, we read this information without batting an eyelid. It's part of our stock-in-trade as Christian believers. But can you imagine the dizzying effect of these ideas on the minds of Jesus' friends?

They have just been told, to their amazement, that the carpenter/teacher of Nazareth *is* the long-awaited Messiah, who is expected to rid their land of foreign rule and triumph over the forces of darkness. In itself this almost incredible idea is more than enough to take on board. But then immediately to cope with the idea that this all-conquering Messiah is no such thing after all but a Suffering Servant who will *die* at the hands of the very religious leaders who ought to welcome him — this is too much.

Too much for Peter too: the difference being that while others kept their astonishment to themselves, Peter must say something.

He took Jesus aside from the others and, for his Lord's sake, began to impart a little advice and, perhaps as he saw it, a little comfort.

'No, no, Lord,' he said (not noticing the contradiction of calling Jesus 'Lord' and then saying 'no' to his wishes), 'this will never happen to you.' The drift is plain. 'You're the Messiah. You'll go in and win. Don't let's have any of this defeatist talk. It'll be OK. Just you see if it isn't.'

Jesus' response was as shattering as it was unexpected. Turning to Peter, he said:

'Out of my sight, Satan! You are a stumbling block to me; you do not have in mind the things of God, but the things of men' (Matthew 16:23).

Peter's jaw dropped and his eyes opened wide. Could he believe his own ears? Here he was, inspired by God himself to recognize Jesus as Messiah. Here he was, helping him along the road to victory and now he was being called Satan to his face. What was so terrible about trying to preserve the Master from harm?

The truth is, of course, that Jesus was not to be the conquering hero-Messiah. He came specifically in order to be the Suffering Servant. Peter's well-meant but thoughtless advice came to Jesus as a vicious temptation to avoid the suffering and the cross, which was why he reacted so sharply to it. The temptation came not from Peter but from the Evil One. So he spoke to Satan, 'Out of my sight!' Poor old Peter happened to be in the way.

Poor old Peter? Within a few minutes it seems, he was uttering truth which was beyond human calculation, emanating from the Father himself; and then being the channel for noxious temptations emerging from the Pit. If one person, as near to the Lord as Peter was, can be subject to communications from above and below as easily as that, we need great care in discerning where *our* ideas are coming from.

How are we to know?

So this question of receiving messages from outside ourselves is not a 'both/and' or 'it just depends how you look at it' problem. As the air is full of radio, TV and satellite signals, so is the spiritual air humming with messages good and bad. Our problem as Christians is how to tune in to the messages which come from God and how to block out the others. Here are seven simple tests to use: seven questions to ask of an idea, suggestion or picture that comes into our minds:

1. Is it biblical? It doesn't have to be couched in old-fashioned language or even to be in the words of a text from the Bible to be biblical. The question is this: is the idea we have in mind in line with what the Bible teaches? If it is clearly out of line, there should be no argument about it (one that suggests itself is making love to someone else's wife/husband. This is obviously forbidden in the

57

Bible). But it may be much less clear-cut. Should I follow an inclination to call on somebody whom I haven't met for some time? Provided it's not the aforesaid wife/husband(!) there's nothing in the Bible which forbids such a course, and, in general, it's a caring and good idea.

Many people get over-sensitive about what is 'biblical'. On the one hand there are those who refuse to do anything unless they can find a precedent in the Bible. On the other are those who excuse all sorts of questionable behaviour by claiming that it is not specifically forbidden in the Bible.

But to think and act 'biblically' means to get to know the Bible more and more as the years go by — and there's no substitute for *reading* it regularly, carefully and prayerfully — and letting its general drift sink into our thinking and our feelings. In the Bible we get to know the God of the Bible. Through these pages we can legitimately ask whether an action might please him or not. To know the Bible is to hold up a mirror to the will of God. This is the first test of whether a communication is from him or not. If it is not against the direction of Scripture our next question to ask of our intended course of action is:

2. Does it follow the teaching of the church? By 'church' we mean both the historic strands of orthodox, central Christian teaching, from the Apostles' Creed onwards, and also the teaching of our own congregation or fellowship, assuming that it bases its doctrines on the Bible.

If the Bible gives me no clear indication whether I should apply for a job in a casino, the church's interpretation of the Bible's message will probably tell me that there are more Christlike ways of getting a living than by presiding over the fleecing of gamblers by means of 'chance' games. Our general knowledge of the Bible's intention should have told us this already but it is always wise to check out any message or guidance we feel we are receiving against the church's approach. The third question is:

3. *Does it inspire encouragement from wise and prayerful friends*? Not all of us have the benefit of a supportive group of prayerful friends but we can all get advice from individuals on matters which are too specific for the Bible's or the church's teaching to decide. 'I feel I am being told to go out with Harriet.' The Bible concordance doesn't have 'Harriet' under 'H' nor do the church's teachings include such an item. But friends who know both you and the young lady concerned may be able to help.

If you have a strong desire to do something, or have an urgent feeling that a course of action should be followed, check it out with prayerful friends. If you are reluctant to do that because you are afraid they will counsel you against it, watch out! Have you a guilty conscience? Be even more determined to discuss it with them.

4. *Is the proposed action loving*? or will someone be hurt as a result? Sometimes, of course, a small hurt is necessary as part of a greater love, but the question here is whether we are being considerate of other people at all. Some Christians seem to receive their guidance and follow it all on their own with no thought of its effect on others. They barge about among their friends (and those who were once their friends) like shoppers in Food Fayre who use their trolleys as battering rams. This is not the way to fulfilling the royal law of love.

5. *Is it what we expected*? This is not a certain guide, but it often happens that we do what is obvious without a nudge from on high. What is not so obvious, something that needs a change of direction from us, something perhaps that seems most unusual, may well be a direction from God.

'Go and speak to that person.'

'But, Lord, that's ridiculous. He's a high-up and I'm only an ordinary sort of chap.'

'Go and speak to him.'

'But Lord, I'm on foot. He's in a state carriage.'

'Go and speak to him.'

'But Lord, I've nothing to say to him.'

For the whole story, if you don't know it already, read Acts 8:26–40.

But again beware. If an odd idea comes to you it is not God speaking just *because* it's bizarre! Check the other guidelines too.

6. Are you ready to obey? Once it is clear to you that the message means something and that it comes from God, are you prepared merely to marvel? Or to get on with it? This is not a test of the truth of the message but it *is* a test of your sincerity.

7. Did it turn out well in the end? This will be a test to apply after your decision has been made. Did you see God's hand in the outcome? Was there a positive step forward? This will not always be obvious, but it's well worth checking up on.

These seven tests will not provide you with a watertight guidance system. They are pointers. They must not be used mechanically or thoughtlessly (or prayerlessly). When each has been considered, stand back and view the whole picture. What we need here is what some people call 'sanctified common sense'. Others call it wisdom.

So we cannot accept every thought, picture or idea that floats into our minds as from God. Ideas come from many sources. We need care in discerning them.

Look back to the account of the prayer group on page 49. How did they measure up to the seven tests in this chapter?

Do you act too quickly on impulses that come to you? Or are you in danger of ignoring the Spirit of God by *never* acting on impulses?

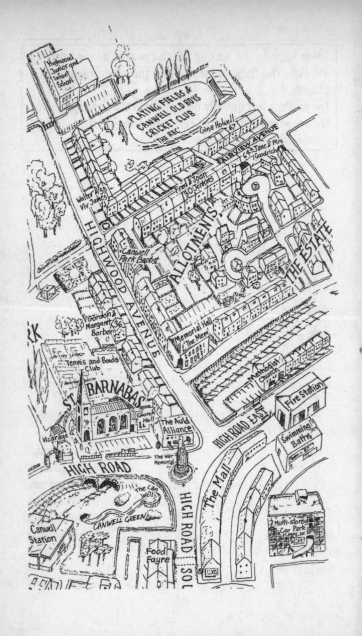

7

Gina's story

Mrs Georgina Annette Holwell (née Crisp); 67 Fairview Avenue, Canwell Park, SW31; widow; age forty-six.

The subject of this history has been introduced elsewhere (see pages 10–11 and *The Barnabas factor*). She is described as dark-haired and full of vigour, wiry and tough, an indefatigable church worker. Her husband, Andrew, had been killed, only a few years previously, in a car accident. She had continued to live in the same house, had quickly found herself a full-time job in the council offices at Canford Heath and had, as they say, 'kept up wonderfully'. She had no children. Her only relation, a cousin, lived in Godalming.

In fact she had 'kept up' much too wonderfully. She had

not allowed herself the luxury of tears or grief of any kind. Having been brought up not to show emotion she believed it to be a sign of weakness and kept any demonstration of feelings strictly under control.

As a result, her relationships and her church work took on a hard-edged quality. She became dogmatic. She over-worked. She 'helped' people who did not wish to be helped. She particularly attached herself to Margaret Barber who was a prey to doubt. Gina had no doubts. Margaret needed only to commit herself fully, to trust the Lord and the Bible, and her problems would roll away. Thus spake Georgina Holwell and thus shrivelled Margaret Barber ('I *have* believed, I *have* trusted, I *am* committed...I think').

'Scandal'

Then had come the Canwell Park scandal. By an odd combination of circumstances, Gordon Barber was seen by old Mrs Goodrich (across the road in Fairview Avenue at number 64) apparently leaving Gina's house early one morning. In fact Gordon had posted some papers through the letter box and was getting into his car as Gina, in her dressing gown, came to the door and waved to him.

All this had been too much for Mrs Goodrich, who loved a scandal, and when her daughter Jane had discovered that Margaret and Shelley Barber had been away for the previous night, the scene was set for rumour to multiply. And multiply it did.

Fortunately the principals in the drama were easy to question and the truth came out quite quickly, to the relief of some, the disappointment of others (including Mrs Goodrich, who never totally believed the true story) and with one or two lasting consequences.

The worst result of the episode was that Gina and Jane, though neighbours and fellow church members, had never spoken to each other again, except in a formal way when necessary. Both had intended to break the silence, but the longer it lasted, the more normal it became and the more difficult the task of breaking it.

The positive outcome of the 'scandal' was that Gina and Margaret became friends and were able to help one another by honestly sharing their shortcomings and feelings of inadequacy. Some of Margaret's doubts had been allayed; some of Gina's hardness softened. All this has been recounted before. All this had been nearly a year ago. In that year much had happened.

'Wholeness for London'

No sooner had Gina begun to find something of her true self and to allow some feelings to surface when she found herself sliding into depression. Gina Holwell *depressed?* Impossible. A sparkling, vigorous, outgoing person. So said the neighbours, but Gina had swallowed her pride and visited her GP.

Several bottles of tablets later the depression was no better. One of her problems was lack of real friends. She was estranged from Jane Goodrich, and with the depression came an unwillingness to continue her visits to Margaret. Margaret assumed that Gina wanted to be left in peace so didn't press her to continue the relationship. On the surface Gina coped. She did her work, like an automaton perhaps, but she did it. She attended the church. She listened to much talk of encouragement and of the example of Barnabas the encourager. And it all washed over and around her and seemed to mean nothing at all. Reaching home she would draw the curtains, switch on the television and gaze with unseeing eyes, hour after hour, at unreal images of unreal people in an unreal world. The indefatigable church worker was defeated at last.

Then came 'Wholeness for London', a preaching and healing campaign with a team of Christians based in a community in the north. For some reason Gina permitted herself to be led to the meeting by the vicar's wife, Diana, but she can't remember getting there or anything that the preacher said. All that she now knows is that she found herself going forward for help at the end of the meeting, that she passed out completely when hands were gently laid on her and that a glorious sense of warmth and peace and reassurance had swept into her.

Moreover, the sense of peace, and with it a sense of the presence of God, did not leave her the next day. Nor the next. She had been open to the influence of the Holy Spirit and he had gently and lovingly flooded her being. The depression waned, not all at once, but within weeks rather than months.

A new Gina emerged, not hard-edged like the original model, but alert again, brimming over with new life and energy once more, 'ransomed, healed, restored, forgiven', and ready to throw herself into the controversy that was by now tearing St Barnabas' Church in two — renewal.

Gina fitted naturally into place as the charismatic (in every sense of the word) leader of the movement for change, for renewal of worship, of people and of the community. Margaret Barber was once again the object of her approaches, not this time in a dogmatic onslaught, but with a loving but insistent call for Margaret to allow herself

66

to be baptized in the Spirit. Diana Monteith was a great help to Gina, praying with her, encouraging her, yet guiding her away from too much flamboyance which would have offended and hurt many people.

So it was that Gina came to be spearheading the group that called for change in the church's furnishings, worship and general direction under the agenda item number six at the church council meeting. And so it was that the church began to take sides. The 'Butterfly Brigade' Cyril Kent called them. The 'Chief of the Fuddy-Duds' they called him. Labels didn't help.

There was no doubt that Gina had experienced a real and wonderfully refreshing and healing event. It was clear to all, even to Cyril, that she was bursting with new life. She exhibited a new confidence, a new purpose and determination to reach even higher levels of commitment and service. In one particular, however, Cyril was right when he shook his head one day over her retreating form and said, 'Appropriate aims but inappropriate self-confidence. She'll come another cropper one of these days.'

Gina's 'cropper'

What Cyril had in mind is not recorded, but Gina's 'cropper' came in a most unexpected fashion.

The 'Gales Week' keynote speaker had been rightly emphatic that Christians ought not to keep the faith to themselves. He drew an impressive picture of Christian failure in this regard — 'ghetto gangs' he called them, Christians who spent all their spare time in each other's company and rarely met people who were not like-minded. The speaker contrasted these 'ghetto gangs' with the Lord himself, who spent so much time in the company of the outcasts of society that he was accused of being a friend of drunkards and sinners.

This emphasis had not been lost on Gina and she had successfully befriended several of her colleagues in the council office. It was no surprise, therefore, when Gina was invited to the leaving party of one of them, a party to be held at 'The Auld Alliance', Canwell Park.

(In case the name of this hostelry arouses interest, it should be explained that the landlord, Murdo MacLeod and his wife, Tinette, hailed from Scotland and France respectively. They had been at school together and had experienced a teenage romance, which had been nicknamed 'Auld Alliance', the traditional alignment of Scotland and France against England. Relying on the public's lack of historical knowledge and its general goodwill they had successfully persuaded the owners of the 'Rose and Crown', Browne Mann Breweries, to change the name, and trade had improved appreciably.)

Goodwill flowed generously, as did the wine, and Gina's earlier decision to drink only bitter lemon had been abandoned. 'Just a small one,' she had said, little suspecting that the buyer of her 'small one' would easily persuade her to have another small one, and even more easily a third. To be fair to her 'benefactor', he didn't know that Gina was still completing her course of anti-depressant tablets.

Thus it befell that at ten to two in the morning the dwellers in Highwood Avenue were awakened to the sound of raucous singing. They were used to a few rowdy songs (most originating from the rugby club dressing room) at closing time, but this was much later than usual and the subject matter of the songs seemed rather unfamiliar:

'Be bold! Be strong for the Lord your God is with you...'

the song broke off into confused gurgles followed by loud laughter.

'Praise ye the Lord. Praised be the name of the Lord...'

There was a loud belch, followed by a wail and a succession of groans. An indignant householder put his head out of the window and beheld a crumpled heap of humanity clinging to the pillar box outside his house.

WPC Horton, and her colleague in the patrol car, showed that night just how positive and helpful the police can be. Gina had been taken to the outpatients department of the General Hospital, examined and found not to be a junkie. Her party clothes suggested that her indiscretions were not necessarily habitual. As she became more lucid she was able to give her address.

At twenty-five minutes to four on that same morning, old Mrs Goodrich, who slept little, was alerted by the reflection of a car's headlights on her ceiling. Sitting up in bed she could see a police car drawn up at Gina's house and an unsteady form between two police officers proceeding towards the front door. Mrs Goodrich's mind began to work quickly. What would Jane make of this? Jane had said that Gina was a new person. They still hadn't made peace with one another but Gina was now 'on fire for the Lord', whatever that meant.

If it meant being escorted home in the early hours of the morning, Mrs Goodrich knew how to make capital out of it.

Mrs Goodrich of course had not heard the choruses and hymns. But Mr Anderson of Highwood Avenue had. *And* he and his wife had carried Gina into their house to await the police. *And* they had discovered her identity. *And* they had not kept the story to themselves the following morning.

How do you react to this story?
Had Gina not really received the Holy Spirit, not properly understood the presence of the Lord?
Or do you think all this talk of healing and renewal is greatly exaggerated, and human beings will always be fallible anyway?
Which view do you feel happier with?
Do you think it's an unlikely story?
If so, read on.

8
Peter's story

We left Simon Peter in chapter 6 feeling rather sorry for himself. He had tried to help Jesus in the best way he could, trying to protect him against the storm that seemed to be gathering, and the Lord had rounded on him and called him 'Satan'.

But then Peter was never one to remain downcast for long. Very soon he was back on form, full of enthusiasm, taking the lead among the disciples, keeping close to Jesus, even as the months passed and the storm-clouds gathered.

Those clouds had now become so dark that it was obvious to all of Jesus' followers that, unless a miracle happened, the end of his life was near. It was Passover week and the Lord had celebrated the solemn meal with the disciples, but with a totally new emphasis, drawing attention to his body and blood which were to be broken and poured out.

Even Peter must have realized by now that Jesus was determined to go through with whatever sacrifice was demanded of him. There was no point in pulling at his sleeve and trying to make him deviate from this purpose. Judas had gone out mysteriously into the darkness and the other eleven disciples felt deeply disturbed. The story is related in Matthew 26:31–75.

The problem for Peter, even more than for the others, was frustration, inactivity. He longed to be in the thick of some programme, some debate, even physical violence if it came to that, but he didn't even know what was in the Lord's mind, except that some great and ominous event was about to unfold. There was therefore only one thing that he and his fellow-disciples could do, and that was to follow Jesus, to stay with him in whatever struggles lay ahead. That, at least, was plain.

Ridiculous!

At this moment, Jesus broke across Peter's thoughts with yet another of his shattering statements:

'This very night you will all fall away on account of me, for it is written: "I will strike the shepherd, and the sheep of the flock will be scattered." '

Had Jesus read his thoughts? But in any case, this was preposterous. 'All fall away'? What had they been doing for three years but following Jesus wherever he went? Surely staying with him now was the only thing they could do. Peter was highly indignant:

'Never mind about the others Lord. Of course what they do is up to them, but I will never leave you. *Nothing* could

72

persuade me to desert you.'

Jesus looked at Peter with a mixture of sorrow and deep sympathy.

'I'll tell you the truth,' he said, 'before the cock crows tomorrow morning, you will have disowned me three times.'

'That's ridiculous!' Peter's blood was up. If he thought at all at that moment he must have assumed that Jesus' words were meant to challenge him and draw out an even greater determination to follow.

'Even if you have to die, Lord, I will die with you. I've nothing to lose. I will never let you down, *never*.' So impressive was Peter's affirmation that the other disciples joined him: 'Never, Lord, never.'

Thus determined, they followed him to the place called Gethsemane, where he prayed in an agony which they were unable to share. Yes, they slept, but at least they stayed with him.

Then Judas reappeared, accompanied by a band of soldiers who arrested Jesus. So *that* was Judas' game! Peter was fully awake now and once again his temper rose to breaking point. He reached for his sword and swung wildly at the nearest of the arresting party. Jesus stepped forward, attended to the victim and quietly commanded Peter to put his sword away. The soldiers then closed ranks around Jesus and marched him off. The gospel writers record his followers' response with unemotional simplicity:

'Then all the disciples deserted him and fled.'

But Peter at least realized what he was doing. ' "I will never desert you." Is that what I said? What am I doing now? This is terrible!'

With a supreme effort, Peter stopped, turned and went back, retracing his steps with a wildly beating heart. Every step was a burden, but he would not desert the Lord. 'Even if I have to die.' He followed the military party to the court-yard of the high priest's house. Jesus was taken inside. Peter was barred from entry. He stood, breathless, not knowing what to do next.

Dawn disaster

What follows is recorded in all four gospels, Matthew 26:69–75; Mark 14:66–72; Luke 22:54–62 and John 18:15–27.

To Peter's surprise, the servant-girl who was on gate duty opened the gate and beckoned him to come in. One of the other disciples carried some influence with the high priest, had already gained admittance and had put in a word for Peter.

'You're to come inside,' said the girl. 'I suppose you're another of Jesus' followers.'

'No I'm not,' said Peter, almost automatically as he made his way into the courtyard.

What had he just said? Well, he'd said it now. It couldn't really matter very much. She was only a slave anyway. No-one of importance. And he probably wouldn't have got in at all if he hadn't told a white lie. What mattered was that he was inside and as near to his Lord as he could be.

There was a fire burning in a brazier at the centre of the open courtyard. The night was cold, and the temple guard, waiting for new orders, together with the servants who had to stay up all night too while these strange events were unfolding, warmed themselves by the fire and chatted about the significance of what was going on.

The gate-girl, going off duty, passed by.

'This man is one of them, you know.'

What *was* this wretched girl playing at? He'd already

told her that he was not a disciple, so he couldn't lose face now, especially before all these other people. With an oath, he denied that he even knew Jesus.

However long was this night going to last? What was going on in the house? Why was Jesus being kept so long? Several times he felt uneasy that he had told people that he didn't know Jesus but he comforted himself that the compromise was the price of staying there.

An hour or so after his second brush with the servant-girl, Peter noticed that the first light of dawn was appearing in the east. He drew this to the attention of the nearest temple guard, with whom he had struck up an acquaintance. As he did so, another guard looked up sharply.

'You're a Galilean, aren't you?' he said. 'You speak with a northern accent.'

Peter's nerves had been drawn almost to breaking point for nearly twenty-four hours with hardly a pause for sleep. Now something snapped. He cursed and swore, 'I don't know Jesus. I've never met him...'

He made such a commotion that the hubbub of talk stopped in the courtyard and everyone paused to hear what was happening. At that very moment, Jesus himself was being led along the colonnade on one side of the courtyard. In the silence a distant cockerel crowed to greet the new day.

The Lord turned and looked straight at Peter.

Then Peter remembered what Jesus had said. He stumbled out, his eyes filled with tears of shame and bewilderment. Simon the Rock had crumbled.

'Betwixt muck and a golden crown'

If Gina Holwell's collapse was a surprise, what about Simon

75

Peter's? Some will say that Pentecost had not yet come and that Peter was to be a changed man. This is true, but he wasn't perfect even then. But that comes later.

Others will point to 1 John 3:6: 'No-one who lives in him keeps on sinning.' Perhaps neither Gina nor Peter were properly 'in him'. But 'sinless perfection' does not fit the biblical picture of God's grace and love, nor does it do justice to experience.

With sorrow and humility we have to acknowledge that we are creatures of the earth, staggering about down here in boots clogged with clay and mud, unable of ourselves even to walk straight; and at the same time we are forgiven children of the Father, adopted by grace into his very family, brothers and sisters of Jesus Christ himself.

G. A. Studdert Kennedy, the 'Woodbine Willie' of the First World War, put these words into the mouth of a 'Tommy', an English soldier in the trenches. They sum up the situation almost to perfection:

> Our Padre, 'e says I'm a sinner,
>   And John Bull says I'm a saint.
> And they're both of them bound to be liars,
>   For I'm neither of them I ain't.
> I'm a man, and a man's a mixture,
>   Right down from 'is very birth,
> Part ov 'im comes from 'eaven,
>   And part ov 'im comes from earth.
> There's nothing in man that's perfect,
>   And nothing that's all complete;
> 'E's nubbat a big beginning,
>   From 'is 'ead to the soles of 'is feet.
> There's summat as draws 'im uppards,
> And summat as drags 'im down,

And the consekence is, 'e wobbles
   'Twixt muck and a golden crown.[1]

The soldier was inaccurate at one point. The Christian
is not 'neither saint nor sinner', but 'both saint and sinner',
as the rest of the verse goes on to express.

Once again two ideas side by side which seem to cancel
each other out. Yet they're both true. There's a missing
dimension which, if only we saw it, would help us to understand the paradox.

Donald MacKay used to put it this way: two people
occupy exactly the same point as defined by a precise grid
reference on a map. Yet they are a mile apart from one
another.

Impossible? Apparently.

But one of them is in an aircraft a mile above the other.
As MacKay says,

> *It simply means that one of them is vertically above
> the other, like aeroplanes 'stacked' before landing.
> One of the first things an airport radar operator
> learns is that two aircraft moving to the same posi-
> tion on the radar screen will not necessarily
> collide!*[2]

Here is a true Christian, sins forgiven, adopted into God's
family, yet still liable to let him down. Why doesn't God

[1] Extract from 'Sinner and Saint: a sermon in a billet' from *Rough
Rhymes of a Padre*, G. A. Studdert Kennedy (Hodder and Stoughton,
1918).

[2] 'What makes a contradiction?' Chapter 4 in *The Open Mind and
Other Essays* by Donald MacKay (Inter-Varsity Press, 1988), p. 39.

prevent his chosen ones from sinning? In other words, what is the third dimension here that will help us to understand this apparent contradiction? What is the aircraft in this equation?

Surely it's this: whether we are Christians or not, all human beings are liable to go wrong, morally. When we are 'born again' (as Jesus described it to Nicodemus in John 3) the distance between ourselves and God is bridged by Jesus; his self-sacrifice makes provision for our wrong-doing; we are forgiven. But we are not perfect. Not yet. Not until that great day when the Lord returns and we are welcomed into his presence for ever.

So we still have free will. We can choose to go wrong — often we seem to go wrong without choosing. We lean that way. The two elements which are apparently contradictory but which are both true are that we remain potential sinners, even when we are forgiven sinners. Paul agonizes over this problem in Romans 7:7–25. It can be a comfort to know that someone as apparently saintly as Paul could have that sort of problem. It will come as no surprise that Simon Peter did too.

How do you account for the vulnerability of Christians? Have you experienced the Holy Spirit personally? Has the experience helped you to be more *stable*? As you read on, ask yourself: how can nose-dives be prevented?

9

Picking up the pieces

How Simon Peter survived the days following his denial of Jesus is not recorded. His tears, his shame, contrition and repentance were all genuine. He stayed with the other disciples after the harrowing day of crucifixion and was on hand to be first into the empty tomb after Jesus rose from death.

The risen Jesus appeared to Peter as well as to the others (1 Corinthians 15:5) but we are not told what passed between them both.

Despite these occasional appearances of their Lord the disciples seemed uneasy and without a clear plan. Why did Jesus not stay with them and establish the new kingdom? His coming to them was wonderful indeed but then he would mysteriously withdraw. Most of them returned to their home ground, Galilee.

Peter, Thomas, Nathanael, James, John and two other disciples were discussing what had happened one evening down by the sea-shore. Some were for taking the initiative and setting up an organization to proclaim the kingdom, others argued for lying low while they waited for Jesus ɔ give them direction. The water lapped against the fishing boats and the familiar smells of the sea-shore moved about them in the evening air.

Suddenly Peter drew a deep breath, stood erect, and announced, 'I'm going fishing again.' (This story is told in John 21.)

After a brief discussion it was agreed that all seven should go together, that very night. After all what was there to lose? Jesus had not forbidden it. And they could do with the money. The boat, long idle, was soon ready for the water and new nets obtained. A thrill of excitement spread through the company. Here was action at last, something they could *do*, something they were familiar with, something they were good at.

Or were they?

Nine long hours later, cold and dispirited, the old firm of skilled fishermen admitted defeat. The thrill of excitement had long departed and numb fingers had time and time again untangled the weed-strewn net and cast it, ever less hopefully, over the side. The result: nothing. Not a single fish in the whole night's work.

As they stretched their aching limbs and looked about them, someone spotted a fire on the shore nearby. A man was tending it. He stood up, his face illuminated by the flames, in the grey dawn. A call came across the hundred yards or so of shallow water:

'Have you caught anything?'

'Not a shrimp.'

'Try the other side.'

Of all unreasonable things this seemed about the most irrational, but they couldn't do any worse than their record so far. So they cast the net one more time.

'It's fouled on the bottom. It won't come up. It moved a bit. It's not fouled. It's *full* of fish. All hands to the net, it's full...'

John was the first to realize who the stranger was.

'It's the Lord,' he said quietly.

Without a word Peter plunged into the water and waded to the shore.

It was a strange breakfast. Jesus already had bread and fish prepared. They added some of their catch and settled down to enjoy the meal, but uncomfortably because no-one had yet acknowledged that this was Jesus. They knew him. They knew that he knew that they knew him. There were awkward silences.

'Feed my sheep'

They finished their meal and were sitting or lying (they hadn't been to bed) around the fire. Jesus spoke very quietly to Peter:

'Simon, son of John, do you truly love me more than these?'

That was hard. Not Simon Peter, the Rock, but back to being merely 'son of John' again. Peter felt suddenly stripped of his rank. And of course he loved Jesus better than all the others did. Didn't he say so? Didn't he...? Didn't he deny that he'd ever met Jesus?

'Yes, Lord,' he answered humbly, 'you know that I love you.'

Then Jesus said a strange thing. No specific word of forgiveness or reinstatement but a charge; 'Feed my lambs.' They got up and walked by the sea-shore.

While Peter was trying to sort out in his confused and sleepless state what this might mean, Jesus spoke again, asking him the same question. Peter answered as before, with perhaps a higher pitch to his voice.

'Take care of my sheep,' said Jesus, 'Do you love me?'

'Do you love me?'

Suddenly Peter woke up to what was happening. A fire in the courtyard and three denials before dawn. Now a fire on the sea-shore at dawn and three questions.

'I don't even know him!'

'Do you love me?'

Peter was amazed. The Lord whom he had betrayed and denied with oaths and cursing had not only received him back without a word of criticism or reproach but was calling on his love and devotion and entrusting him with the task of shepherding the flock that he was so soon to leave behind. Jesus was still speaking, warning Peter of hard times to come, hinting at the supreme honour and ultimate ghastliness — crucifixion. He concluded his time with Peter with the simple words, 'Follow me.'

Peter was back in his old place — restored as a leader and a shepherd. If that can happen to Peter then there's hope for Gina Holwell, and for me, and for you...

Not *Gina*!

A recent innovation at St Barnabas', Canwell Park, was the 'counselling service'. The phrase had a double meaning. It was a service to the church and it took place during and after the evening service. Those who needed help of any kind could go to the front of the church at the close of the service, a prayer was offered for them and they could then move into a quiet corner with a 'counsellor' (half-a-dozen members had been trained for this function) and receive such help as could be provided. The hard cases were then referred to the vicar!

This practice was predictably welcomed by the progressives and deplored as 'new-fangled psychological nonsense' by Cyril Kent and his friends. One of these, however, Margaret Barber, had joined the scheme. A year ago she had had a series of discussions with Gina Holwell and, as a result, had been encouraged to take a counselling course through the extension studies department of a Bible college.

So it befell that, on the evening after Gina's night out, a counselling service was to be held. In order to please as many people as possible Timothy held an 'Evensong' according to the Book of Common Prayer, 1662, and the two didn't really mix. Neither did it please anybody: the traditionalists complained about the counselling and the progressives complained about the Prayer Book. Timothy sighed as he began with the time honoured words, 'Dearly beloved, the Scripture moveth us in sundry places...'

His eye detected a movement. An ashen-faced Gina Holwell, wearing dark glasses, had crept in at the back of the church. By now of course everybody had heard about what had happened. Few expected her to be there. Some said she would never darken the doors of the church again. Most thought she should be left alone, but Diana had called briefly in the afternoon with some words of comfort and a flask of coffee. Timothy's mind wandered from what he was saying to what he would say to Gina:

'...to the end that we may obtain forgiveness of the

same...shall I leave it all to Diana, perhaps that would be best...wherefore I pray and beseech you, as many as are here present...on the other hand, she would think it's a bit off if I ignore her. I *am* the vicar after all...unto the throne of the heavenly grace...'

As it happened Timothy did not get to speak personally to Gina that day.

When the time came for the 'ministry', as some called it, Cyril led the way out of the church, followed by half-a-dozen or so others. At the same time, Gina Holwell walked steadily and purposefully to the front and stood, head bowed, facing Timothy.

A hush fell upon the congregation. 'Not Gina. Surely not *Gina!*' The thought ran silently to and fro. Gina was a leader in the church. She was the one who had encouraged all the others to get involved in counselling. She was usually the one who was on call to help those in trouble. And now she was publicly admitting her own need of help. The situation was the more dramatic because, unusually, no-one else came forward, so Gina stood alone.

Fred Jenkins had buried his face in his hands. Gina had been filled with the Spirit. She'd been healed of her depression. She was the leader of the renewal group. And now this. Someone was going to say 'I told you so.' He could hardly bear it.

His wife Joan leaned across and whispered in his ear, 'I told you so,' she said.

By a supreme effort of will, Fred clamped his jaws together and buried his face deeper in his hands.

The way back

The prayer had been said and the final hymn was being

sung. Gina looked up to see who would be counselling her. There, smiling faintly stood...Margaret Barber.

The coincidence was almost too much. It was the kind of thing that only happened in books, not in real life. All Gina could manage by way of communicating her thoughts was a flood of almost uncontrollable tears.

Timothy decided to leave well alone and turned his attention to other people.

Margaret stayed with Gina for what seemed like half the night, but was in fact forty-five minutes, took her home and arranged to see her again the following evening.

When she arrived, after a day at the office, which had proved difficult to say the least, Gina seemed relaxed and almost her old self again. The act of walking to the front of the church had been for her a public confession of guilt. The words of the prayer had assured her that, however far a Christian falls, he or she can be picked up and carried on by the Lord until they are ready to walk again. There was still a great deal to talk and pray about, but the highest hurdle had been overcome already.

Hardly had coffee been drunk and biscuits eaten than the apparition in the white nightdress appeared at the door.

'Shelley, you're supposed to be *asleep*.'

'But I heard you and Auntie Gina, so I came to see her. Can I see her for a minute Mummy?'

Shelley's eyes were so large and appealing that Margaret said, 'Well, yes, just for a minute then,' and Shelley and Gina were exchanging a hug.

'Have you been naughty, Auntie Gina?' said Shelley.

'Shelley dear, how many times have I told you not to be rude to grown-ups,' Margaret spoke wearily as one who had little hope of being obeyed. But Gina was equal to the situation:

'Yes I have been naughty, Shelley. And I'm very sorry for it.'

'I was naughty,' said Shelley, 'I put sand in the engine of Daddy's car and it didn't go. I didn't *mean* to do it. I just did it. And I was sorry too. And do you know what Timothy said?'

'Mr Monteith,' said Margaret sharply.

'Timothy,' said Shelley again, but more loudly, 'said that Simon Peter had done the worst ever thing you could do. And *that* was...'

'Hurry up, dear!'

'And *that* was to tell people he didn't know Jesus, when he *did* really. And you told us all about Peter and how he was forgiven as well. And Timothy said that if Peter could be forgiven then so could I, if I was really sorry. So you can be forgiven as well, Auntie Gina.'

Shelley had another hug before she finally climbed the stairs for the last time that day.

It's odd that Jesus never said anything about the lambs feeding their shepherd.

Is any act so evil that it cannot be forgiven?
If so, what is it? Why?
What does Jesus have to say on the subject (Matthew 12:30–32)?

To plan or not to plan

'**H**ow long does it take you to prepare a sermon, Timothy?'

Jane Goodrich had called on Fred and Joan Jenkins, with the excuse of returning a cookery book, but really because she wanted an hour or so out of earshot of her mother's complaints. Her mother was now ninety-five and one couldn't condemn her for complaining but it was a little wearing when you heard it all the time. The Jenkinses were 'within range'. That is, they lived sixteen houses down Fairview Avenue from the Goodriches and old Mrs Goodrich 'allowed' Jane to go that far and no further, except on church business when Jane insisted. Jane did sometimes go further but her mother didn't 'allow' it.

When she arrived, Jane found Timothy and Diana

drinking coffee ('If I had a pound for every cup of coffee the members of this church drink I'd be a millionaire before I'm seventy,' thought Jane) and had been persuaded to join them.

In half an hour they disposed of the latest public pronouncements of a northern bishop and the most recent scandal about films portraying the sex-life of Jesus. Then Jane took the opportunity to ask the question she had been wanting to ask for a long time: 'How long does it take you to prepare a sermon?'

'Not as long as it ought to,' said Timothy quickly. 'When I was at college I was told that I should spend at least ten hours in preparation for each sermon. I suppose I don't usually manage more than three or four, sometimes only one or two.'

'But you put in a lot of thinking round them, dear,' said Diana, not wanting anyone to think that her husband was being lazy, 'and a life-time of experience and reading,' she added for good measure. She looked nervously at Fred, whose eyes were opening more and more widely.

'Stand up and spout'

'Ten *hours*?' said Fred incredulously. 'That's more than a quarter of the working week!'

'Speak for yourself,' said Timothy under his breath, but only Diana heard him.

'If you had three sermons to prepare, you wouldn't be able to do anything else at all.'

'Well, I don't usually have more than two, and, as I said, I don't spend as much time on them as I should. There are too many other things, and people, mostly people, to deal with.'

'Exactly,' said Fred, leaning forward. 'You could use those three or four, or six or eight hours visiting people in hospital or calling on the shut-ins, the people who are always complaining that they never see anyone from the church. "I'm from the church," I say to them. "Oh yes, that's all very well," they say, "but I expect the *vicar*." They want to see *you*, you see.'

Diana was on the defensive again:

'But he visits both the hospitals every week, and if he spent any more time calling on people I should never see him at all. Besides, his reading and preparation for sermons are a chance for him to recharge his spiritual batteries. You get very run down with all these wearing people who want things all the time.'

'The Holy Spirit will recharge your batteries,' said Fred. 'There's no need for all this dry-as-dust study business. All you need is the Spirit. "He will guide you into all truth." You told us that in a sermon last year, Vicar, and I've remembered it.'

'Surely he does guide us,' said Timothy, 'but that doesn't mean that I have no responsibility to prepare what he wants me to say so that I can say it clearly and well.'

'But you don't!' said Fred.

'*Fred*!' said Joan.

'What I mean is, you don't improve the message by stewing it over books. Let it come freely. Let the Spirit have his way. Here's another bit of Scripture for you: "Do not worry about what to say or how to say it. At that time you will be given what to say, for it will not be you speaking, but the Spirit of your Father speaking through you." Matthew 10:19.'

Fred sat back and folded his arms as if in triumph.

'Pray before you go into the pulpit that you will be

filled with the Spirit and then just stand up and spout,' he said.

'I do see what you mean,' said Timothy, 'but I can't agree that Jesus was talking about preaching sermons in that bit of Matthew you quoted. You missed out the first part of the sentence. Jesus actually said...' Timothy had pulled out his pocket Bible and was flicking over the leaves, ' "When they *arrest* you, do not worry about what to say." He was talking about times of persecution when people are suddenly hauled up before magistrates to explain their behaviour. There's no need to have a carefully rehearsed speech to defend yourself then. But it doesn't mean that the Spirit can't inspire me to *prepare* as well as to spout as you put it.'

'Well, you vicars have always got an answer for everything,' said Fred grumpily.

'But what about Jesus?' Diana was on Fred's side now. 'He spoke to the crowds whenever he had the opportunity. Surely he didn't prepare sermons and have them in his pocket in case he met a congregation. He spoke when the need arose.'

'But Jesus was different surely,' Jane sounded dubious. 'He was the Son of God, so he knew it all already.'

'Oh I don't know about that,' said Fred. 'He was the Son of God, yes, but he didn't know it all. He was open to the Spirit.'

'Jesus also planned things very carefully,' said Timothy. 'Before he chose his twelve disciples he stayed up all night in prayer. Now what proportion of his working week was that? And when he sent them out to visit the towns and villages, he gave them very precise instructions about clothing, equipment, what to say, how long to stay and all the rest of it. It's all in this same chapter of Matthew.

90

He didn't just say, "Do what the Spirit tells you on each occasion." No doubt he expected them to be ready for special guidance when special problems or opportunities arose, but it was all within a well-planned framework.'

'And your friend Simon Peter was always acting on the spur of the moment and getting it wrong wasn't he?' Joan revealed that she wasn't always as ignorant as she liked to appear and went for more coffee.

Target: Malchus

Immediately after the conversation, when Jesus predicted Peter's denial (described in chapter 8) the Lord made some unusual observations (see Luke 22;35–38).

'When I sent you out to visit the towns and villages, you had a minimum of equipment, but you didn't lack anything did you?'

'No,' the disciples answered.

'Now it's different,' said Jesus. 'If you have money, bring it with you, you will need it. Bring your belongings with you. And if you don't have a sword, sell your shirt and buy one. There's conflict ahead.'

It seems that, as so often happened, Jesus was speaking in picture-language, emphasizing that the times of peaceful ministry were over and a crisis of major proportions was now upon them. The disciples took him literally.

'We've got two swords between us,' they said.

'That is enough,' said Jesus. Was it in sorrow because they had misunderstood him? We cannot hear the tone of his voice. At all events, this was how Peter came to be wearing a sword when Jesus returned from his agonized prayer in the Garden of Gethsemane. The story is recorded for us by Matthew (26:47–56), Mark (14:43–50), Luke

(22:47–53) and John (18:1–11).

Peter and the other disciples had been sleeping heavily. It was pitch dark. Suddenly there was a confusion of voices and the flashing of lanterns and the flaring of torches between the trees. A whole company of temple guards, armed with swords and clubs, was trampling through the undergrowth, apparently towards Jesus and his companions. If they were looking for Jesus, as suddenly seemed likely, how did they know where to find him?

The answer came swiftly. A voice called out, 'Here he is!' It was a familiar voice. The voice of Judas in the darkness. Suddenly the form of the traitor loomed close and he made straight for Jesus.

'Judas!' Jesus spoke calmly, 'Are you going to betray the Son of Man with a kiss?'

Then the soldiers were all round them, far more than were needed to arrest the Prince of Peace and his followers. One of them blundered into Peter as he stood wondering what to do. Without further thought, Peter whipped out his sword and heard it whistle through the air as he aimed a murderous blow at his assailant. He hit something in the dark and the man cried out in pain. Jesus was there in a moment.

'No more of this,' he said to Peter, 'Put your sword away.' He was already kneeling beside the wounded man, who was bleeding profusely from a mutilated ear. Jesus performed his last recorded act of physical healing, and allowed himself to be led away to execution...

'Murderous.' That's a tough word to describe Peter's rash intention. We are familiar with the story of Peter, the sword and how he cut off Malchus' ear. Nice bit of swordsmanship that! Teach a soldier a lesson without actually endangering his life.

But can we really believe that even an Olympic fencer could accurately slice off the ear of a moving man, in broad daylight? It's possible perhaps. But Peter was no Olympic fencer; he was a fisherman. And it was pitch dark! No, he was aiming at the *man*, perhaps in the general direction of his head. It was more by luck than judgment that he failed to kill Malchus. Luck? It depends what you mean by luck.

Recipe for chaos?

Fred Jenkins was not to be moved from his opinion that in the life of the Spirit-filled Christian there was little room for careful preparation. Peter was his hero. What if he did have a swing at the soldier? At least he was a man of action. At least he did something. The others all ran away. God needs courageous activists like Peter much more than he needs dry-as-dust theologians, who think all the right thoughts and then run away in a crisis. Besides, Jesus came and healed the man didn't he? That's just the point. We may make mistakes, but God overrules them so we've no need to worry.

Jane said that she thought Fred was being totally irresponsible and that his ideas were a recipe for chaos. Diana was giving more instances of how people had acted when prompted by the Spirit and had seen remarkable things happen. Timothy was smiling to himself and awaiting the opportunity to leave for home. Joan was asleep.

At number 64 up the road old Mrs Goodrich cleared her throat, looked closely at her clock again and drummed her fingers on the bedside table.

At last, Timothy took his chance to break in and sum up the discussion. He didn't doubt for a moment, he said, that the true Christian was under the minute-by-minute control of the Spirit of God. (Fred snorted but Timothy took no notice and went on.) This did not mean that the Christian had no responsibility to think about what he believed and what he was doing, to prepare properly in advance and to use his common sense when he lacked specific leading. It was yet another case of 'both/and'.

Being filled with the Spirit and under his guidance didn't excuse the Christian from preparing what to say. Being prepared and well-organized didn't prevent the Christian from being suddenly, even spectacularly, moved to depart from the planned course of action.

The problem, once again, was to know when it was the Spirit of God speaking and when it was the impetuous voice of self (or the exaggerated conscience making over-the-top demands and pretending to speak in the name of God. We knew who was pulling that one, didn't we?). And when we knew it *was* God speaking, were we ready to obey? Practice made perfect.

So Timothy summed up their discussion, Joan woke up in time to say goodbye, and the debate, in one form or another, went on, and on, and on...

Does God speak to you? How?
When did you last obey him?
Have you got the balance between planning and spontaneity about right?

11

Anger: for and against

There can be little doubt that when Peter struck out at Malchus he was a very angry man. Peter seems to have been a man of violent emotion; intensely loyal, idealistic, capable of great love and, as is the case with many emotional people, who live as it were in technicolour, capable too of great anger.

Is anger right for the Christian?

Cyril Kent and his generation were brought up to believe that anger should be always avoided, suppressed, denied. It was a sign of weakness to be angry. Anger demanded repentance.

Fred Jenkins and his friends, however, could see another side to the subject. There had been a seminar at 'Gales Week' on righteous anger, entitled 'Be angry and sin not.'

He had come away with the mistaken idea that anger was a good thing, provided you really meant it.

Margaret Barber had also studied anger, somewhat more deeply, as part of her counselling course, and could see both points of view.

'Do not let the sun go down...'

Margaret listened to Cyril and Fred arguing about anger one Sunday morning. They *both* seemed quite angry! She reflected how this aspect of behaviour was forming yet another watershed between the traditional views and the 'renewed' ideas of the progressives. 'Keep the lid on' seemed to be the motto of the old brigade: 'Let it all hang out', that of the new. She took out her file after lunch and, between bouts of Junior Scrabble with Shelley, tried to clarify her mind on the subject.

The essay she had written was based on Ephesians 4:26–27:

> *'In your anger do not sin': Do not let the sun go down while you are still angry, and do not give the devil a foothold.*

That first phrase was a quotation from Psalm 4:4 which put it in a slightly different light:

> *In your anger do not sin;*
> *when you are on your beds,*
> *Search your hearts and be*
> *silent.*

It didn't say that it was wrong to be angry. It was no more

wrong to feel anger than to be tempted. It was what you *did* with your anger, how you handled it, that mattered.

Peter was not condemned for his anger. The Psalmists seemed able to get angry, even with God, and still made a niche for themselves in Scripture. Anger was one of God's own attributes anyway, according to David:

> *'O Lord, do not rebuke me in*
> > *your anger*
> > *or discipline me in your*
> > *wrath.'* (Psalm 6:1)

Jesus too was angry when he made a whip of cords and drove the money-changers out of the temple (one version is in Matthew 21:12–13). Paul certainly seemed to hint that appropriate anger was in order, provided it didn't turn into the wrong thing and give a foothold to Satan.

So there are two kinds of anger. The right kind, which finds its origin in the wrath of God, and the wrong kind, which opens the door to a Visitor from Below.

'The wrath of God.' Those words, taken at face value, give quite the wrong impression. Wrath seems to imply violence, as if God loses his temper, becomes purple in the face and stamps his foot in fury. But this is not the meaning of the phrase at all. It means the unwavering opposition that a loving and holy God must feel and show towards everything that is destructive, hateful and rebellious. 'Righteous indignation' we might call it, but even that already dilutes the idea.

Jesus demonstrated his Father's 'wrath' when he cleansed the temple. He may have got warm in the process but he does not seem to have lost control of himself.

This kind of burning yet controlled anger is what we

should all feel against injustice and sin in all its forms. 'Be angry and do not sin.' Let your anger be of this kind.

But the anger we fall for much more often is the loss of temper, the flaring of emotion because injustice has been directed at *us* (or we feel it has). There's no use trying to sit on this kind of anger. Drive it down inside and it becomes resentment and resentment turns to bitterness and is one of the causes of depression (Margaret made a mental note to check her 'depression' file next week).

It may be necessary to give vent to anger — to shout, to take violent exercise (preferably not with a drawn sword!). But two principles apply: the first is, try not to hurt someone else in the expression of your anger. Shout at God if you like, as the Psalmists did. It won't hurt him and you will soon see the ridiculousness of it. But many people are easily hurt by our expressions of anger. They may explode in response, but they may withdraw and nurse resentment in their turn. Avoid hurting other people if possible.

The second principle is to give it time to cool. Paul suggests a maximum of twelve hours — sort it out before bedtime. David, the shepherd, was a nocturnal animal, so suggested 'When you are on your beds, search your hearts and be silent'. Paul, the activist, probably slept as soon as his head hit the pillow (or jail floor). David, the reflective, perhaps suffered from insomnia. Either way, let there be *time* for the peace of God to flow in again.

And, as a postscript, repent. Yes, Cyril was right in this. No human anger is ever really righteous through and through. It leaves a nasty taste behind. It has hurt pride and self-centredness mixed up in it. So repent, turn round and face the other way. Receive God's forgiveness and feel quite different. Because you *are*.

The Littlehampton saga

Every year, since the heady days of the 'charabanc', St Barnabas' Church had arranged an outing to Littlehampton. It had begun as a choir outing in the 1930s, was revived after the Second World War, and now nobody seemed to want to discontinue it.

The weather had been good this year and fifty-four people, in high spirits, boarded the coach for home at 6.30. The teenagers bundled their way to the back seats, wielding bags of crisps and bottles of Coke, and they were followed by a small contingent of senior citizens from 'The Haven'. They had all come with Mrs Beesley, who had been on the first ever Littlehampton outing as a member of the choir, and who regarded it as her special occasion.

The rest found their seats among like-minded friends and the automatic door sealed them in.

The student of group dynamics would have distinguished five groups: the teenagers, the old people, the traditionalists at the front of the coach, the progressives in the middle — and the driver, who was uncommitted but in ultimate control.

As usual it was not long before someone started to sing. Some of the youngsters could be heard over the sound of the engine, singing a song from the charts, which made some of the old folk sitting in front of them turn round and stare. Gordon Barber decided that something more organized would be better, something they could all join in with. So he called everyone to order and soon had them singing four-part rounds and hearty but meaningless songs that he had learned round the camp-fire in his scouting days.

After two or three songs of the 'yup-I-dee-I-dah' variety

and 'Green grow the rushes–O', Fred and his daughter Carol could be seen talking to one another. As the song finished Fred stood up and announced a chorus from 'Gales Praise'. The group around Fred sang lustily and jangled keys at appropriate moments and several other people joined in half-heartedly without really knowing the tune or the words. Most were silent.

Gordon found himself most unreasonably annoyed. He sat down, with a set expression on his face and stared straight ahead. Why must Fred always muscle in on what was already going well? He knew Fred's reason for setting up a rival option. Fred thought that Gordon was unspiritual. These nonsense songs were not right for a group of Christians. But not everyone there was Christian. To sing praise to God would be a powerful witness. That was Fred's line. But Gordon saw things differently. This was a day out, not a mission. Surely Christians should be able to let their hair down a bit and not always have to sing pious songs? Besides it was no 'witness' to sing songs which the outsiders didn't know. In fact it turned them into outsiders and made them embarrassed. Gordon clenched his teeth and as the 'Hallelujah' rang out for the seventh and last time he jumped to his feet again and led a vigorous four-part rendering of 'London's burning'.

This, of course, was the cue for Fred to get in immediately with a long and complicated 'Gales Praise' song which was sung right through five times and would have gone on if Gordon hadn't interrupted to announce 'Clementine'. Next time round, however, Fred and his side did not allow themselves to be interrupted but went doggedly on, singing the same chorus over and over again, while Gordon and his team competed staunchly with several more songs.

At first this seemed like good fun, but the noise level

increased rapidly and tempers were beginning to fray. The business was getting out of hand. Both sides were competing to drown each other out, and to add to the confusion the young people at the back added their heavy rock contribution to the general chaos.

Connie Bassett to the rescue

By now most people were getting angry, not least Gordon and Fred, and nobody seemed willing to make the first move to bring about peace and quiet.

At this point two things happened independently but simultaneously.

The driver stopped the coach.

And Connie Bassett stood up.

Connie Bassett was an elderly lady of mountainous proportions. She had come from London's East End dockland and rumour had it that she had been 'an entertainer'. She didn't come to church, except at Christmas and harvest festival, but she was a friend of Mrs Beesley's and lived down the corridor from her in 'The Haven'.

As the bus stopped so did the singing. The driver was about to tell his passengers that he couldn't concentrate with all this noise, and traffic conditions were difficult, but Connie Bassett got in first. Towering above everyone, not only in person but in righteous indignation, she addressed the company, in broad Cockney which it would be improper to reduce to writing:

'I come today,' she began impressively, 'for a nice quiet day by the seaside. An' up to now I've enjoyed meself. But you lot ought to be ashamed. I thought you was Christians till about half an hour ago. An' now I 'ave me doubts. Anyway I think we'll 'ave a change. You lot keep quiet an' I'll sing to *you*. Drive on driver. This'll soothe you down an' captivate yer 'eart deary. Be careful you don't go to sleep.'

The driver realized that the situation was now under control and good-humouredly engaged first gear. But he need have had no fear of falling asleep.

Connie took a deep breath, which inflated her ample bosom even further, and sang. It wouldn't have made much difference if people *had* been singing in opposition. Her voice, like herself, was enormous. Her claim to have been an entertainer was clearly no idle boast. She was used to filling a music hall with sound (without the benefit of amplification) and a small space like a coach was as nothing to her.

'Come, come, come and make eyes at me down at the old Bull and Bush, tarararara...'

Fred ducked involuntarily. This was worse than 'Green grow the rushes–O'. Gordon looked very sheepish. Most of the passengers were taken so completely by surprise by the turn of events that they listened open-mouthed.

'My old man said "Follow the van and don't dilly-dally on the way" ' was followed by 'I've got a lovely bunch of coconuts' and within a few minutes some were joining in. By the time they reached Canwell Park, the final 'Oi' of 'Doing the Lambeth walk' made passers-by turn to see what was happening.

'Thanks Connie,' said Gordon, as they climbed down to the pavement. Squeezing Connie in and out of the coach had been quite a task and they were all now breathless but on firm ground.

'That's OK sweetheart,' said Connie, depositing a huge kiss on the forehead of the astonished church treasurer. 'Let me know when you want me again. Peacemaker *extra-*

102

ordinary, that's me.' Taking Mrs Beesley's arm, she waddled away towards 'The Haven'.

'God works in mysterious ways, Fred.' Gordon, Margaret, Fred, Joan and Carol were walking up Highwood Avenue.

'She made mincemeat of us, didn't she?' said Fred ruefully. 'I'm sorry about that, Gordon. It was my fault you know.'

'It takes two to make an argument,' said Gordon gallantly, conscious that what he said wasn't very profound.

'It took about fifty-two,' said Joan.

'We all got angry,' said Margaret, 'but you know Connie's anger was the right kind. She was angry because we were being so stupid. Her anger was Christ-like and *she's* the one some would say wasn't a Christian. It makes you wonder.'

Next morning at breakfast, Shelley Barber was curious.

'Daddy,' she said, 'why were you singing "Come and make eyes at me" in the bathroom?'

Gordon opened his eyes very wide and wriggled his eyebrows which always made Shelley helpless with mirth. She never got her answer.

Are you afraid of anger? Yours? Other people's?
Do you agree that there can be good and bad anger?
How do you tell the difference?

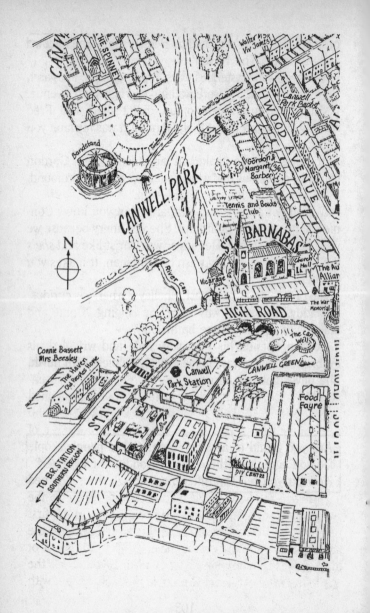

12

Pentecost

Jerusalem was teeming with people. Everyone who lived in or near the city seemed to be in the streets or cramming the ways leading to the temple. Even so they seemed to be outnumbered by the vast crowd of pilgrims who had converged on the Holy City from every corner of the known world, everywhere that is, where Jewish people lived.

For these were all Jews, either exiles who had returned for the festival or converts who had been grafted into the chosen race and were visiting Jerusalem, some for the first time. For all that they were Jews they were speaking the language of their present homeland. The confusion of tongues was reminiscent of Babel itself. If you asked the way to the Pool of Siloam you would probably be met with an apologetic shrug and a few words in Greek, 'I'm sorry, I don't live here.'

It was Pentecost.

No, not an English Bank Holiday, formerly called Whitsuntide. This was basically the Jewish harvest festival, fifty days after the beginning of Passover ('Pentecost' comes from the Greek word, meaning 'fifty'). But it was not a village festival. At this time every male was required to present himself at the sanctuary, hence the flocking of pilgrims to Jerusalem. As well as thanksgiving for harvest, thanksgiving for the provision of the Law on Mount Sinai had been added to the festivities, so there is no wonder that Jerusalem was awash with excited holiday-makers. It was a compulsory day out:

> *On that same day you are to proclaim a sacred*
> *assembly and do no regular work. This is to*
> *be a lasting ordinance for the generations to*
> *come* (Leviticus 23:21).

Nine o'clock in the morning

Peter and the other disciples were there too, of course, but they still felt that strange mixture of flatness and excitement, hope and lack of purpose. The meeting with the Lord by the lakeside had promised to be a new beginning, but then Jesus had left them again. The discussion about returning to the fishing business had been resumed. Some said the amazing catch was a sign that they should start up again: others that the lack of natural success overnight was a sign that they should not. Neither had they forgotten Jesus' word, 'wait'.

They had come to Jerusalem for the feast and had seen

Jesus again, this time in an astonishing farewell, just a few days ago. Again he had promised them the Holy Spirit, and power, and he had commanded them to take the good news of faith to Jerusalem, Judaea, Samaria and to the ends of the earth. And *then*...he had left them. They had found themselves looking into the sky. Did he *really* go that way?

So their excitement that something was about to happen was balanced by their deep sadness at losing their Lord — he really did seem to have gone for good this time. And what did it all mean?

Before making their way up to the temple, the friends of Jesus did what they always did when they were together, gathered for prayer at nine o'clock in the morning. They met in the familiar upper room which was large enough to accommodate many more than the twelve apostles. Apart from the general excitement of a festival everything seemed perfectly normal.

Then, without the least warning, it happened. A strong wind got up and blew noisily round the building. This was odd because the weather was clear and the morning calm. The wind thundered in the chimney and became violent so that the whole building seemed to shake. The disciples looked up in fear and somebody noticed that the trees outside were not moving.

What happened next they could never explain. First one then another seemed to be glowing with light, as if a flame had settled on them. Someone cried out in astonishment. An overwhelming consciousness of God's loving and powerful presence took hold of them all. Their faces were radiant. As they exchanged greetings (their morning prayers were now forgotten) they found themselves shouting with delight, 'Hallelujah', 'Praise the Lord!' Then first one, then another

107

called out in another language. Words came to them from...from where they did not know, but they were wonderful words, words which gave glory to God in the highest.

Now the disciples had gone into the house openly, not in secret, but few had taken any notice of them. They always met in the morning, these Jesus people. But the deafening roar of 'wind' had been heard outside as well as in, and in a very short time, a large crowd had gathered to see what was happening, expecting a fire at the very least.

Their astonishment knew no bounds when the friends of Jesus came out, talking loudly and praising God. That in itself was a little odd and over-enthusiastic at this time of the day, but what was amazing was that the pilgrims from overseas heard their own languages being spoken. What a joy for the tongue-tied foreigner who has heard nothing but a babel of voices ever since he arrived, to hear his dear old native language again, and in praise of God too!

Those who knew the disciples were not quite so surprised. 'So this is the coming of the Holy Spirit,' they said, 'this is what they were waiting for.' Others, who did not know them and were, in any case, embarrassed by the whole business, began to laugh. 'They're tight as owls, drunk as lords. I know the kind of spirits that have that effect...'

'Get up and walk'

Peter was on his feet in a moment.

'Drunk, you say?' he pointed at his accusers. 'At this time of the morning!' A round of laughter from the other bystanders and an attempt at a cheer. This was a great beginning to the day!

'No,' said Peter, 'this is what the prophet Joel was looking forward to. Don't you remember, "In the last days, God says, I will pour out my Spirit on all people" (Joel 2:28)...'

Peter was in full flood now, quoting from prophets and psalms, recalling the history of Israel, showing how it all pointed to Christ and his resurrection and how the promised Holy Spirit would come.

The other disciples looked at one another. Was this Peter? Simon Peter? The man who had sworn (literally) that he didn't even know Jesus? Peter the fisherman, but now Peter the orator? He had thousands of them listening, eating out of his hand. Most amazing of all, Peter the blunderer, the buffoon, had been speaking now for fifteen minutes and hadn't said a word out of place. When would he blow it? When would the terrible gaffe come? But Peter went smoothly on and on. He blew it not, neither was there any gaffe.

He finished his speech and paused for breath. Someone called out, 'What shall we do then?'

'Repent and be baptized, all of you,' said Peter instantly, 'receive forgiveness and also this gift of the Holy Spirit that we have just been privileged to receive.'

There followed the busiest Pentecost any of the disciples could remember. By the end of it, when they compared notes they discovered that between them they had counselled and baptized no fewer than three thousand people. All in one day.

Surely it had all been worth waiting for.

There was no thought of returning to fishing now. Every day people were joining the new young church. Many new disciples sold their possessions and distributed the proceeds to those in need. They met daily, praised and prayed, celebrated the death and rising of their Lord in bread and wine, preached the good news openly and boldly and saw wonderful healings and miraculous signs following on. All of this, and more, is described in Acts 2. Chapter 3 goes on to give an example of what was happening.

Peter and John were walking towards the temple at three o'clock one afternoon, the time for afternoon praise, when they passed a handicapped man. This was an everyday event. Jerusalem was full of the halt, the maimed, the blind and the crippled. The temple was their favourite haunt. They had no source of revenue except the begging bowl. Their relatives or friends, if they had any, would carry them there in the morning and carry them away again, with such meagre income as had come their way, in the evening. Those going to the temple might at least have consciences and give more readily than people going to market.

On this occasion, the same man was in the same place. He had been there ever since he could remember. He had been born this way. He knew no other. Automatically and in a droning voice, staring straight in front of him, he called out for money from the two shadows hurrying by.

One of them stopped. The other paused and came back.

Simon Peter spoke: 'Look up!'

The beggar looked up hopefully for the first time that day. How much might he expect? They looked reasonably well off.

'I, like you, possess nothing,' said Peter, 'but I do have something better than money for you. In the name of Jesus Christ of Nazareth, get up and walk.'

Predictably the man stared at them. This was lunacy. Of course he couldn't get up and *walk*. He only wanted a little cash. John too looked uncomfortable. This was a bit too bold, even for Peter. They'd look jolly silly now, with this man sitting there and staring at them. A crowd was already gathering. Crowds always did.

'Come on, John, give him a hand. He needs help you know. He's not in training.'

So John found himself holding one arm, while Peter took the other, and the beggar hung there for a moment, suspended between them. Then he placed one foot gingerly on the ground. And then the other. He rested his weight on them. He moved, very slowly, like a novice on an ice-rink.

Then he fell over.

A groan from the crowd, sadness from some, derision from others, but there was a new light in the beggar's eyes now. Waving away further help he actually leapt to his feet and walked steadily for several yards. Then back again. Gathering his strength he jumped into the air. Applause broke out. The beggar, his face wreathed with smiles, ran back to Peter and John and embraced them both.

Peter disentangled himself from the enthusiasm of the erstwhile cripple and turned to the crowd.

'Men of Israel,' he said, 'why are you so surprised?'

He was off again. Numbers at the afternoon praise in the temple were down that day but applications for the kingdom of heaven showed a marked increase.

Something special and one-off

Timothy Monteith, pastor, vicar and leader of his flock, lay prostrate on the sand. The sun poured into his tired limbs and a gentle breeze was caressing his back. The sound of the waves and the occasional, mercifully distant, shout of a child, played an ideal accompaniment. He felt as if he was suspended between earth and heaven, and wondered vaguely whether heaven included summer

111

holidays. Suddenly he became aware of a voice.

'Darling, are you asleep?'

'Not now.'

'Oh, I'm sorry, but I'm afraid your back will burn if you stay there much longer.'

'Yes. I suppose you're right.' He levered himself up and met the concerned eyes of his wife who was brandishing a tube of sunburn lotion. Then he gladly lay down again and submitted to a gentle massage with the cooling cream.

'Do you suppose that baptism in the Spirit feels at all like this?' said Timothy.

The massage stopped, and then began again.

'Yes. I think it was for me,' said Diana, 'but I thought you didn't believe in it.'

'I can't refuse to believe in people's experiences,' said Timothy. 'I only said that I don't like the phrase used when it only means a special one-off second blessing. You know what I mean.'

'Yes. I know what you mean. But something special and one-off happened to Peter at Pentecost didn't it?'

'Of course, but that was a unique, not-to-be-repeated one-off. The birthday of the church.'

'Who says it wasn't to be repeated?'

'Don't rub too hard,' said Timothy wincing. 'I think I did lie a bit too long. Well, perhaps we really do have time to talk about it all in the next few days. No meetings, no telephone, no funerals, no weddings...Will heaven be like this?'

'In heaven there won't be arguments about the Holy Spirit,' said Diana, 'but, yes, perhaps we can talk about it properly now we're away.'

So they did.

When you think about that Pentecost, does it seem real to you?
Have you, or someone you know, ever experienced anything similar?
How do you account for the change in Simon Peter?

13

Spiritual pains in the neck

'So come on, convince me about baptism in the Spirit,' said Timothy.

Apart from some soreness about the back, they were both feeling relaxed and well. The weather had changed and a strong wind was blowing, but it was dry and clear so they had decided on a cliff-top walk.

'But you're an ordained minister. Surely I don't need to tell you about such things.'

'I'm not ordained while I'm on holiday,' said Timothy firmly. 'Dog-collar's on the wardrobe shelf. I'm just me. Now I believe as well as anyone that a Christian can't *be* a Christian without the Holy Spirit. Paul says that in Romans 8:9. My problem, as you very well know, is that what seems like half the congregation seem to believe that at St Barnabas' Pentecost would solve all our problems. The other half seem to believe that Pentecost was the cause of the problems in the first place and we'd have been better off without it.'

'Well all right,' said Diana, 'Let's take the trads.'

'Mentioning no names.'

'Mentioning no names, of course,' said Diana, eyeing her husband with amusement. 'You may well be right to say that they are Christians, most of them anyway, and that they have the Holy Spirit in their hearts. But why does he stay there, lurking in their hearts? There's no evidence that I can see. It may be true but it may also be a bit of theological algebra.'

'Oh, that's unfair!' said Timothy. 'Just think of people like...'

'Mentioning no names of course,' said Diana, dodging to avoid a blow from a tuft of heather Timothy was carrying.

'Well, just think of the love and the joy and the peace of some of those people. This is all fruit of the Spirit.'

'Fruit, yes, but what about gifts? Where are the evangelists, healers, miracle workers, prophets and all the rest? Where are the tongues we read about in Acts?'

'Are you saying that these people aren't Christians?'

'No,' said Diana firmly, 'I'm saying that if the Spirit lives in them I'd expect to see some more evidence.'

Danger to the church

'OK', said Timothy. 'Let's look at it the other way round. Here's someone, naming no names, who is wonderfully converted, goes to a "Gales Week" and is zapped.'

'Now *you're* being unfair. "Zapped" is a very loaded way of talking about something very special.'

115

'All right, he is greatly blessed. He probably receives some of the gifts of the Spirit, perhaps only one, I don't know, but he is lacking in the other direction. He has no fruit. A chap who goes around laying hands on people and healing them is fine, but if he has no love, joy and patience and all the rest, well, Paul says in 1 Corinthians 13 he's just like an empty drum that somebody's banging. In fact I'd go further, and say that someone who has gifts and no fruit is a positive danger to the church. Those with fruit and no gifts are at least keeping reasonably quiet.'

'You're exaggerating all this,' said Diana defensively.

'Yes, because we're talking in generalities and naming no names. Let me name a name. Fred. Now he has a whole lot of growing up to do? The coming of the Holy Spirit doesn't make people perfect all at once. He lights them up and turns them round and fills them, like Simon Peter. But Peter wasn't perfect even after Pentecost.'

'True. I mean, not that you should have been there. Uncle's funeral was more important. But true that Fred is not perfect. But neither is Gordon. And before you quote Gina at me (since we are naming names now) aren't we just saying that nobody's perfect and that we all have a lot of growing up to do. The coming of the Holy Spirit doesn't make people perfect all at once. He lights them up and turns them round and fills them, like Simon Peter. But Peter wasn't perfect even after Pentecost.'

'OK,' said Timothy, looking at his wife,'let's look at the New Testament, which is where we ought to be looking.' When you came to think about it, Diana really was a very attractive woman. The wind was whipping her curly brown hair away from her face and was giving her a heightened colour. And when she spoke or smiled she showed a lovely even set of teeth. And she was tall and slim. He was a very

116

lucky man, no not lucky, he didn't believe in luck, very blessed. Why didn't he appreciate her more? Too busy. Too much involved in trying to help other people's wives to pay proper attention to his own...

'Tim!'

'Yes dear.'

'Where are you?'

'I'm here of course. I was just giving myself time to admire you.'

Diana's colour heightened a little more. 'Bless you,' she said and squeezed his hand. 'But we were about to start on the New Testament.'

'So we were,' said Timothy, 'You set us all to rights. We were talking about Peter, so let's take the book of Acts. That's where it all seems to happen. I challenge anyone to find a pattern there, let alone in the gospels and letters, that lays down conversion first and a second blessing of the Spirit afterwards. It happened with some people who had never been told about the Holy Spirit (Acts 19:1–7), but they hadn't believed in Christ properly anyway — they'd only heard half a gospel from John the Baptist.'

'No, I agree that there are no rules about it, but everyone in the New Testament, after Pentecost, *assumed* that Christians were filled with the Spirit. Nowadays the 'pentecostalist' or 'charismatic' is talked of as if he or she is an exception to the rule...'

'And they talk about themselves as special people,' said Timothy.

'Well, sometimes. But my point is that the *ordinary* Christian of the early church was what we would call a charismatic. It was the exception to find people, like the Samaritans, who received a special Spirit baptism. Christians didn't need it. They had the Spirit already. It's only after nearly 2,000 years of formality and cooling down that the Spirit has had to return, in the past thirty years, to bring us back to what we should be. So there's no need for a "second blessing" provided people have had the first one.'

'On the other hand,' said Timothy, 'there's no limit to the number of experiences God may wish to give to someone, first, second, third, hundredth.'

'Exactly,' Diana was becoming more and more animated, and more and more beautiful, thought Timothy, 'so if people were taught to receive the Spirit when they come to faith many of our problems would be solved.'

'Hey, wait a minute, you can't instil the Spirit of God by teaching. He is a free agent. Jesus said he is like the wind. He comes when he likes. This was the problem in the past with confirmation in the Church of England. People were told that when the bishop laid his hands on them the Spirit would come in. Then, if they felt nothing, they reckoned he hadn't and were let down. Confirmation was the great passing out ceremony. People never came back.'

'No. I don't mean that you can make him come. Who was it who said, "the Holy Spirit comes like a dove but we can't put him in a pigeon-hole"?'

What is a Christian?

'We're probably back to the question of what a Christian is,' said Timothy, fumbling in his pocket and producing his pocket Bible.

'I thought you'd left all that behind,' said Diana, 'with the dog-collar.'

'Oh, no, I've left my job behind but I'm still a Christian

I hope,' said Timothy laughing, 'I just wanted to check that verse from Acts 2, the sermon that Peter preached at Pentecost. I think he summarized it very neatly. Here we are, Acts 2:38.' He stopped to check the wild fluttering of the pages.

'Yes, here we are: "Peter replied, 'Repent and be baptised, every one of you, in the name of Jesus Christ for the forgiveness of your sins. And you will receive the gift of the Holy Spirit.' "

'So it looks as if there are three elements to the normal Christian experience — repentance, turning round in sorrow for living a life of separation from God; baptism, the sign of God's forgiveness, washing away the sin; and the sign of our commitment and filling with the Holy Spirit, the presence and power of God, bringing gifts and producing fruit.'

'I'll go along with that,' said Diana, after pausing to think about it.

'But it doesn't say that those things must all happen in any particular order, nor that they must all happen simultaneously.'

'Well they couldn't.'

'Exactly. As long as they are there all is well. I suppose ideally a person believes first, is baptized second and receives the Spirit as he rises from the water, as Jesus did.'

'But you baptize babies.'

'Quite. I don't think the order is important. Baptism first, belief and the Spirit later. So some people may need a baptism in the Spirit, as you want to call it, but others may have the Spirit already. In fact all Christians have — it's back to the question of whether he is being allowed to be active in our lives or not. But being filled with the Spirit is a continuous thing. Paul's words in Ephesians 5:18

119

mean, "go on being filled with the Spirit". We just have to wait and let it all happen.'

'Well all right,' said Diana, 'I'll accept your general idea, though it all sounds a bit woolly to me...'

'No, not woolly,' Timothy struck in, 'it's a mystery you see. It's one of those "both/and" situations, not cut and dried.'

'I knew you'd say that. But where we don't yet agree is about this waiting for things to happen. This is where it comes down to practical matters at St Barnabas'. If we don't publicly encourage renewal from the top, the church will remain confused.'

'But there are two problems, as you very well know.' Timothy often said, 'as you very well know' when he was feeling rather annoyed.

'One is that Jesus said the Spirit was sovereign, like the wind, and he decides when to come. The other is that Jesus said, "wait until the Spirit comes". He'll come when he's ready. In the meantime he's here already. Some people talk as if the church that hasn't experienced a big renewal is a purely godless club.'

'All right,' said Diana, putting her arm through Timothy's, 'it's time we enjoyed the scenery. As soon as you start saying "as you very well know" our discussion becomes an argument.'

Timothy drew a deep breath to defend himself with, but decided that Diana looked more beautiful than ever and turned it into a sneeze.

Is the Holy Spirit present in your life?
How do you know?
Do you have spiritual gifts?
How do you rate on 'fruit'? Check Galatians 5:22–23.

14
No miracles please: they're untidy

Several weeks after the Monteiths returned from their holiday Timothy announced that there would be an experimental healing service in the church. Diana smiled a little private smile but thought it best not to say anything, except to be generally encouraging.

The news produced predictable responses from, 'Hallelujah! the vicar's converted', to acid remarks such as, 'We shall need a committee to decide what to do with the discarded crutches.'

The format was to be similar to that of the counselling service. Those who wanted prayer and the laying on of hands could come to the front and kneel, while the ministers prayed with each of them, asking them whether they wanted prayer for other people too (especially for those who were too ill to attend). The ministers included a visiting speaker, much experienced in the healing ministry, Timothy himself, his wife and Gordon Barber. As an elder, Cyril Kent had been invited to assist but had declined on the grounds that he was suffering from a particularly painful boil on the back of his neck.

Joy and disappointment

The service was a cheerful and positive one, with plenty of singing and an explanation of the ministry of healing from the visiting speaker. God, he said, did not wish us to be ill. It was wrong to say that God willed deformities, pain and suffering. Jesus spent much of his time healing the sick and so gave an example to his church. The prayer offered in faith will make the sick person well (James 5:15), he said, and the Lord will raise him up. Of course God did not heal everyone on demand. There might be a lack in our faith; or a sin in our life; or it might be that God says 'wait', but there is no doubt that God wants us well.

Jane Goodrich listened with suppressed but mounting excitement. She felt that these words were meant specially for her. Nothing had ever seemed specially for her before. Ever since she could remember her mother had been the centre of family attention. Her mother was an invalid. Her mother bore great suffering. Her mother expected others to pay attention to her. And Jane had paid attention, patiently, year after year, constantly on call.

When there is an invalid in the family, others are expected to remain fit and well. Any mention of an indisposition is met with, at worst, derision, or at best, with patient resignation. 'Be grateful that you're not in my position, dear.' So Jane could never mention her own increasing difficulties with arthritis to her mother and had not felt able to talk to anyone else either. When she winced, as she often did nowadays, her mother pretended not to notice.

So Jane had been looking forward to this service ever since she had heard about it. She had taken her courage in both twisted hands and had discussed it with Diana. Diana had met her several times, prayed with her, discussed the problem with her and generally encouraged her to expect a breakthrough. So Jane genuinely expected healing. Her faith was buoyant.

Twenty or thirty people took the opportunity of asking for prayer. Several very elderly people from 'The Haven' came specially for the service and were escorted to the front. One or two returned to their seats with shining faces. No sticks or crutches were thrown away but something good had clearly happened to these people. Among the more able bodied came none other than Connie Bassett, the last person on earth, thought Jane, to be expected at this sort of service, even to *any* sort of service. But Connie seemed to know exactly what to do and was steering a tiny soul, who appeared less than half her size and was whispering very loudly in encouragement, 'Come on dearie, you can't come to no 'arm you know. Jesus loves yer. The reverend said so didn' 'e?'

The minute person almost disappeared as she knelt down and had to be hoisted up again by Connie, who seemed to radiate goodwill. She guided her little charge back to her pew and presided over her like a huge hen with a brood of chickens.

Jane was at the front now, her heart beating faster. What would happen? Would she feel tingling warmth all over? Or see a vision? She became aware of Edith Kent asking prayer for her husband and his painful boil. She prayed silently for Cyril. Then someone's hands were laid on her head (she had her eyes closed so she didn't know whose they were). Heavy they seemed but not threatening. The visiting speaker it was who prayed for her most sympathetically and earnestly, that she would receive healing and never be troubled with arthritis again.

She felt an increase of pain in her hands. This must be how it works. It has to get worse before it gets better. She walked unsteadily back to her seat. Her eyes filled with tears. No warmth, no tingling, no vision. Just pain in her hands. Was her faith lacking? Was there some sin in her life? Diana had been so encouraging. And it was the healing expert who had prayed for her. What was happening?

Nothing it seemed. Just nothing. It was as if God had played a cruel joke on her. Here were these other people, glowing and smiling and here was she in tears.

By mistake

Over coffee after the service Jane was able to unburden some of her problems to Diana and to Margaret Barber who was always, these days, on hand to help. Before they had made much progress, however, the little group was split open by Connie Bassett, who burst in on them, dragging her friend with her.

' 'Ere, be introduced! This is Mabel. She's been 'ealed, 'aven't you Mabel? Tell them about it, Mabel.'

Poor Mabel seemed totally at a loss for words, largely because Connie was still hovering over her like a gigantic mother bird, but she finally managed to tell them that she was convinced that her arthritis was better. Jane, warmhearted as ever, embraced Mabel and told her how very delighted she was. Mabel was rendered finally and completely speechless by this approach from a total stranger who came, with tears in her eyes and hugged her. Connie therefore spoke on her behalf. At some length.

When she paused for breath, Margaret asked her the question they all wanted to ask; What had brought her to church? She didn't usually come.

'The 'ealing dear,' said Connie simply. 'I've got no use for churches where they talk about helping others and sing about miracles. I like it where they *do* it. It 'appened to me forty years ago so why not to Mabel?'

'You've been healed?' said Diana hopefully, expecting to hear about the cure of a headache.

'Terminal cancer,' bellowed Connie. 'The quack give me a month to live. It went out the window. Never 'ad a 'int of it since. Bloomin' miracle the quack said. And 'e was right.'

'Who prayed for you?' asked Diana, amazed.

'Canon George.'

'Canon *George*! But he didn't have a healing ministry.'

'So you say, my dear. I don't know what 'e 'ad but 'e prayed for me at me bedside, about to glide orf to kingdom come and 'ere I am forty years later, as fit as a — fiddle.'

Connie used an adjective to describe the fiddle which was not often heard in St Barnabas' Church, but the account she had given was a tonic to them all.

Meanwhile, across the park at 25 Park Avenue, Cyril Kent was sitting in his favourite armchair and blinking in astonishment. His boil had disappeared. There was no trace of it. No trace whatever.

He had been very troubled about the new healing service. He believed that God had the best in mind for everyone whether that involved sickness or health. He made frequent reference to Paul's 'thorn in the flesh', something physically wrong with the apostle, who describes in 2 Corinthians 12 how he had prayed earnestly for its removal. Yet God had seen fit to leave him unhealed. 'My grace is sufficient for you,' he had said to Paul, 'for my power is made perfect in weakness.'

Of course God *could* heal — he was all-powerful. But usually he used doctors, nurses and hospitals. These healing services could so easily get out of hand. People imagined things. They got over-emotional. Especially those young girls, Carol, Sharon and Rachel. And all this physical healing business detracted from the real purpose of the church, which was to preach the gospel of salvation from *sin*, not from disease.

Cyril had argued these things with himself, in his chair, ever since Edith had left for church. He felt lonely. He had to admit it. His wife had deserted him just when he was feeling particularly low and had gone to a *healing* service. It was too bad. He felt very sorry for himself.

Then, gradually, a peace began to creep over him. He realized that the throbbing pain of his boil was getting worse because he was so tense and resentful. He relaxed his grip on the arms of the chair. He recollected that these resentful thoughts would not be what his Father in heaven expected of him. He asked forgiveness and experienced the warmth of the knowledge that he was an adopted member of God's family.

At St Barnabas' Church Edith was asking prayer for her husband. So was Jane.

Cyril felt almost as if he had been to sleep for a long and refreshing night's rest, though the clock told him that he had closed his eyes for only three or four minutes. He got up with a feeling of unusual lightness. Instinctively he

127

felt tenderly the back of his neck, to pat the dressing on his boil. The dressing was still in place. The boil was not. Gingerly he removed the plaster. There was no sign of the boil.

He sat down again, rather suddenly. But he didn't *believe* in this kind of thing! Was this God's sense of humour? And what would he say to Edith? For an awkward moment he almost wished he had his boil back again. Then he remembered how painful it had been and thanked God for its going.

We cannot scrute them

For once the Vicarage telephone had been silent for a whole mealtime, and on the Wednesday following the healing service, Diana and Timothy were back to their discussion of the Holy Spirit.

'I can only explain this sudden "baptism in the Spirit" as you call it,' said Timothy, 'in terms of something like 2 Timothy 1:6, "Fan into flame the gift of God, which is in you through the laying on of my hands." All Christians have the Holy Spirit, but he needs to be fanned into flame.'

'You make him sound like a mindless fire,' said his wife, wrinkling her nose.

'Yes, and fire does get out of hand,' said Timothy. 'The Spirit comes in power and does miracles, and people get excited and it starts a band-wagon effect. They expect more miracles and sometimes they manage to counterfeit them — oh yes, all innocently. A healer is expected to heal. If he doesn't deliver the goods he loses respect so there's a pressure on him to find someone in the audience with a sore big toe or an aching back (there are always plenty of them).

128

'So on the one hand there are people who are intoxicated with the Spirit and we almost wish he hadn't started them off, and on the other hand people who are terrified of the whole business and say it must be satanic. God wouldn't act like this. No miracles please, they're untidy!

'Look at what happened on Sunday. Poor old Jane, praying to be relieved of her arthritis and all we can comfort her with is 2 Corinthians 12:9. And there's old Cyril, complaining like mad that we dare to have a healing service and he gets healed by mistake, it seems to me.

'What is God playing at? It was well said that his ways are inscrutable. We cannot scrute them. It really does *look* as if the Spirit is mindless fire. Read about what happened in Wesley's time or Jonathan Edwards' or today with John Wimber. People falling about like ninepins. Some wonderful healings and conversions and some people put off for life. If the Spirit is sovereign why isn't he more careful with the fragile china?'

Diana thought for a while.

'I suppose we have to choose between quenching the Spirit (if you can really quench a divine fire) and trying to co-operate with the Lord of power. To follow where he leads, or to put up the shutters.'

Timothy smiled.

'In that case I know which it has to be,' he said.

When people have odd and apparently supernatural experiences, can we distinguish between the work of the Spirit, the devil and the human mind?
How?

15

'No, Lord, no! It's against my religion'

Healing, and the absence of healing, is another of those both/and, either/or questions that appear at every turn.

On the one hand it is clear that God does not set out to harm the people that he loves. Jesus emphasized healing in his own ministry and also urged his people to ask for *anything* in his name and he would do it (John 14:14). James, too, promised that the prayer of faith will make the sick person well (James 5:15). 'Ask and it will be given to you,' said Jesus (Matthew 7:7).

And it is clear that people *are* healed. There can be no doubt that the healing of Cyril's boil, Mabel's arthritis, Connie's cancer even, have many parallels in modern life, as they had in the life of the early church. Thus far the case for healing seems watertight.

And yet...

And yet, there are people, full of faith, who have sought healing with tears but never seem to find it. The apostle Paul was one of them. Cyril was right when he said that sin is a greater problem for the human race than disease. And it is a very short step from feeling full of faith and asking great things from God to expecting instant healing on demand and telling almighty God what to do!

No, God will not be pushed around. He is sovereign. Yet for some extraordinary reason he responds to our prayers. But not like a slot machine, not automatically. He is personal, not a mindless fire, even if it looks that way sometimes.

In the end we have to admit that we face a mystery here. It is our duty and our joy to pray for the sick but we must beware of giving God the orders. Unless we are given the specific gift of faith we cannot *know* that a person will be healed as we could wish. Sometimes they are. Sometimes they're not. He is Lord. Our place is to worship and wonder. 'Your will be done' expresses not faithlessness but humility.

Visions on an empty stomach

Another area of confusion is the conflict between 'religious' views of what is right and wrong, and the authentic voice of God, which sometimes cuts across them.

Religious people are always in danger of fixing limits to the extent of God's grace, usually just a little beyond where they see themselves to be, so that many others are excluded. We recall the jibe, sadly not far from the truth in some cases, concerning the Christian who said, 'They're an unbelieving lot at our church. In fact, only two of us are really soundly converted — me and the Pastor. And I'm not too sure about the Pastor either.'

The New Testament Jews, of course, had no doubt that they were the chosen people. God had made it clear to them, from Abraham onwards. For them that meant that God had rejected the *goyim*, the other races, the Gentiles. Despite many broad hints in the Old Testament that God's love knows no bounds, the Hebrews could not imagine that the Gentiles could be favoured with salvation. The early Christians were Hebrews. Their preaching was to other Hebrews. Even at Pentecost, the people who heard the disciples were Jews.

The mould had to be broken, but the minds of the members of the young church were closed. So God moved in. He chose a Roman centurion, Cornelius, a God-fearing and devout man who commanded a cohort in the Italian Regiment stationed at Caesarea.

And he chose an apostle. Guess who? Simon Peter. And he brought them together in a most remarkable manner, described in detail in Acts 10.

An angel appeared distinctly to Cornelius and told him to send for Simon Peter, who was staying in the seaside town of Joppa at the time, and he would learn something to his advantage.

Meanwhile, totally unsuspecting, Peter was stretching his faith and his tolerance to the limits by staying with another Simon, Simon the tanner. Not only is tanning a peculiarly smelly business but, for the strict Jew, forbidden, because contact with the corpses of animals made one ceremonially unclean (Numbers 19:11–13).

Presumably Simon the tanner was responding to the good news of Jesus, so Peter was staying at his house. One day, when the sun was highest in the heavens, Peter went up to the roof-top to pray. The afternoon meal was not yet due, although delicious smells of cooking drifted up from the oven in the centre of the open courtyard. Peter composed himself to be patient and to use the time in the best way he knew how, in prayer.

The flat roof was the quietest place available. There was little fear of being disturbed (except by the smells from the courtyard which were so much nicer than the stench of the tanning works). Peter adjusted the poles which held up the sun-shelter, a sheet of sail-cloth to give shade from the burning sun.

He settled down to pray.

He closed his eyes and his mind filled up with images of sunshine and sail-cloth, liturgy and lunch, prayer and pepper. The picture cleared.

He became aware of the sail-cloth awning, not fixed on poles any more, but being lowered before him as if on a crane suspended from sky-hooks. He had been down at the dockside that morning, watching the loading of a merchant ship. But the merchandise swung on the derricks in the harbour was quite unlike the contents of this awning. It was full of animals! All kinds of four-footed animals, as well as reptiles and birds. And with the vision, a voice:

'Get up Peter. Choose meat. Kill something and eat it.'

The idea was absolutely abhorrent to Peter. He'd had quite enough of the smell of decomposing animals in the tannery and he was not anxious to shed blood anyway. But far worse than either of these considerations was the fact that many of these creatures were ceremonially unclean. The word of God, in Leviticus, made it quite clear that the Lord forbade his people to eat such creatures.

'No, surely not Lord,' said Peter impulsively. 'I have never

133

sinned by eating unclean flesh. I'd rather go hungry.'

The vision was repeated. Peter wondered whether he was dreaming, seeing a revelation or experiencing a horrible nightmare. How could God, the Lord who made the rules, demand that his servant should break them?

'No, Lord, no! It's against my religion.'

'Peter. Don't call anything unclean that I have made clean.'

'Lord, no.'

Once more the awning filled with animals swung low over Peter's head as his mind was torn apart by his desire to obey the God of the old law and the God of the new spirit. The chains seemed to be rattling as the crane lowered the sheet. The shouts of the dockside mingled with the thumping of the pulleys...

And he awoke.

Someone was hammering on the courtyard gate and shouting to attract attention. Three men from Caesarea, thirty miles away, had come at the command of Centurion Cornelius to ask for one Simon Peter. Was he here?

Peter's first thought was that he was to be arrested again. Trials? Prison? Death this time? Was that the meaning of the vision? How could it be? He sat still while the debate at the gateway went on. Then it came to him, he never knew how. It could only have been the Spirit of God speaking to him. 'Get up and go down to these men. And go with them. I have sent them.'

So Peter took his courage to the limit and presented himself at the gate. Instead of demanding entry and talking of arrest, here were two civilians and a soldier, telling him of their master who was a God-fearer, respected by the Jews. And he'd met an angel. A Roman centurion had had an interview with an angel?

Peter flung open the courtyard gate.

'Come in, and welcome,' he said, 'I think a meal is on the way.'

Folk-religion

'It's against my religion.' It is fatally easy to shelter behind that idea and use it as an excuse for stopping our ears to the authentic voice of God.

In this sense our religion (literally the word means 'rule of life', 'system of faith and worship' from a Latin word which meant 'bond' or 'obligation'), means the set principles that we observe, often unconsciously, believing them to be right and good, as they often are, yet sometimes forming a barrier to new ideas from God himself.

There is a remnant of folk-religion, alive and well in our villages, yes and even our cities, within and without our churches: Live a decent life, it tells us; go to church sometimes; 'read our Bibles' occasionally; 'say our prayers' often; lend a hand at the fête; give to charity sometimes; don't gamble (much); don't get drunk (too often — we can't all be perfect); don't talk about the occasional sexual infidelity (it's not polite in religious circles) and always smile in public. One might go on.

This is the religion of the post-Christian era which Satan loves to encourage. It deadens us to the authentic faith, like an inoculation which gives a mild dose to prevent the real thing.

But let those who have escaped from this olde world religion of our grandparents cease to feel smug. There's a new version available. This one is the same as the other but it has different labels.

Go to a church which is lively (plenty of singing in the

modern idiom); raise your hands in worship (close your eyes if you're too shy to raise your hands); read the Bible when you *feel* inclined; pray when the Spirit moves you (if you pray at other times it might be false); live in freedom and honesty; eat well, drink well and if you do commit adultery, admit it freely, especially at 'Gales Week'. 'You *have* been to "Gales Week" haven't you?'

Both of these folk-religions, as described here, are exaggerated. But not too wildly so. And there are other forms of folk-religion too, much subtler than these.

If God calls me to abandon my cosy system, how do I respond? 'No Lord, no. It's against my religion'?

The 'Walkman factor'

Timothy had preached on Acts 10, Peter and his roof-top vision. God was calling us to a new dimension of faith. The new wine of spiritual life must replace the old, habitual forms of folk-religion. The dry bones must come together and exhibit life. The lame man must be healed and leap and walk (Timothy did overdo his illustrations a bit, but they knew what he meant).

At least they thought they knew what he meant.

Margaret Barber had heard him saying, 'Listen to the voice of God inside you and ignore the faith of your ancestors,' and she winced.

Cyril Kent had heard him saying, 'Abandon the Scriptures and look to feelings for your guide,' and he shuddered.

Fred Jenkins had heard him saying, 'Let's be a bit less formal in our ways of doing things but don't get too charismatic,' and he smiled wearily.

Mrs Beesley had heard him saying, 'Make the services

longer and sing more choruses,' and she had longed for Canon George.

Connie Bassett had heard him saying, 'Be more honest in your religion and enjoy it,' and she had grinned broadly.

Diana had heard him being very courageous and she had smiled inwardly and thanked God for him.

Each had heard what he or she had expected to hear or feared to hear. They had brought their own 'Walkman' receiver inside their heads, and the sermon had been filtered through their own preconceived ideas.

The 'both/and' of true faith and lifestyle being woven together was too much for most of them to grasp and their suspicions of what he might be getting at deafened them to what he was really saying.

Look back at the two folk-religions on pages 134–135. Take a deep breath and honestly describe your own. Do you like what you see? Have you been ruthlessly honest?

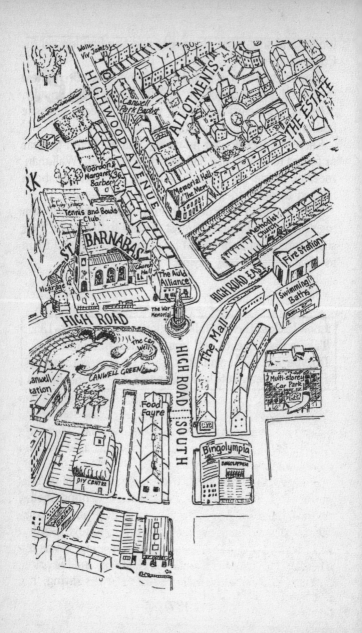

16
Public stance: private behaviour

Gina Holwell and Margaret Barber had met frequently since Gina's dramatic 'accident' as she liked to call it. But they both knew that the accident had not been entirely accidental. The strain between public stance and private behaviour had reached breaking point. There are reasons for it and those reasons can be brought out and examined and sometimes changed.

Shelley was in bed (after the usual pantomime of 'seeing Auntie Gina' and Auntie Gina's complimenting Shelley on how her new teeth were growing, a nicely-judged comment which sent Shelley into a delirium of joy). Gordon was involved in a standing committee meeting. It was the Tuesday after Timothy's sermon about Peter and his vision.

'Yes, I know what he *means*,' Margaret was saying, 'but

it's what he implies that worries me. This listening to God business, new wine, throw the old religion away, can be very dangerous. You know what can happen when you just listen to God. You start listening to your own ideas and you justify them by saying, "God told me to do it." I don't mean *you*, Gina, I mean people do.'

Gina had heard all this many times before.

'It's not right to throw away all the safeguards, Margaret, you know I agree with you. God's words today will be in line with his word in the Bible and his wisdom through his people through the ages...'

'But Peter was told to disobey the Bible. It's very confusing.'

'Well, yes. He didn't know what we know now, that the old machinery of laws and regulations were being superseded by the new regime of grace. But that kind of revolutionary change, on *that* scale, can't happen today.'

'Some people seem to think that the new "age of the Spirit" is doing away with everything that has ever gone before us.'

'Yes, Margaret,' said Gina, 'but some people are wrong. I hope you don't still class me as one of those "some people".'

'No, I'll give you the benefit of the doubt,' said Margaret. 'Tea or coffee?'

Why the fear?

'The real problem, as I see it,' said Margaret, after they had settled the cups, saucers and biscuits ('go on, they're quite small'), 'is this business of public stance and private behaviour. You know the Pharisees' thing of having two standards.'

140

'I don't think the good Pharisees did have two standards actually,' said Gina, 'but if I accept your definition, yes, I have been pharisaical.'

'Gina, I didn't mean you. I wasn't talking about you.'

'Yes, but we *are* talking about me. My public stance was "be filled with the Spirit and be a great witness for Christ". My private behaviour left a lot to be desired. The two didn't match.'

'But that was a one-off,' said Margaret. 'People have forgotten about it and you have been forgiven by them and by God.'

'I've been forgiven by God, but people haven't forgotten about it. Especially old Mrs Goodrich. The curtain moves and the beady eye looks at me. All hours of the day and night. It's the eye of my conscience. And I'm not sure about the "one-off". It could happen again you know, in that or some other way.'

'What do you think is behind it all then?' asked Margaret, settling herself more comfortably.

There was a long silence, broken only by the thudding of Shelley's feet as she ran to the bathroom. Margaret took no notice. At length Gina spoke again:

'I think it all goes back again to the question of fear.'

There was another pause.

'*You* were always the one who was afraid I remember. You were terrified that Gordon would have a road accident.'

'I still am.'

'Well, maybe, but at least that's fear of something real. I used to think that I had no fears at all. Andrew really did die in a road accident. After that I thought that there couldn't be anything worse. There was nothing more in life to be afraid of. So I see now that I was putting on the fearless act.

'Then I remember one morning, after church, groups of people were talking and I was left out. I admit now that I was very jealous. There really was no reason why I had to be included but they all seemed so happy together and I was an odd one out. So I went home in a temper and I think I cried for half the afternoon.'

'Oh *Gina*!'

'Well I can tell you now. It was over a year ago. It was after that silly business about Gordon. I wasn't speaking to Jane...'

'Are you now?'

'No. No I haven't got that far yet. Anyway I felt torn in two. I wanted to be with people and I didn't. Then came all the excitement of the Spirit-baptism and the depression and the healing and then my starting to put pressure on you again. Why do I do it? And what am I so afraid of?'

'I don't know anyone who has been through so much trauma as you have, Gina, I really don't. All those things have happened in the space of a few years, most of them in the last year or so. No wonder you're a bit mixed up.'

'Mixed up yes, but why the fear?'

'I'll tell you what I think if you like.'

'Please do.'

'You won't be shocked?'

'I can stand anything.'

'I've heard that before,' said Margaret wryly.

'Well, OK, I'll try.'

'I think you fear relationships, close relationships.'

'But that's ridiculous,' said Gina, at once. 'That's just the thing I've *wanted*.'

'If what you fear and what you want are the same thing you are in deep water. And I think this is what has happened. Since Andrew died you have longed for a deep

142

relationship, to take the place of Andrew, but you have feared to get deeply involved with *anyone* — not only the opposite sex — because you were afraid of being hurt again. So you came over as aggressive and hard at first. That has been much better since...since "Wholeness for London" but you haven't really made much progress in relationships. You still haven't spoken to Jane. Your need for close relationships came out in that party. *And* of course the tension between your longing for someone close and your keeping everyone at arms' length probably contributed to the depression, if it didn't actually cause it.

'The depression was healed but the tension came out in other ways. The fear you have is a fear of closeness to people and even though you exchanged depression for a binge, the fear remains.

'There. That's exactly what a counsellor should not do. I've told you what I think instead of asking you the questions. Now you'd better tell me where I've got it all wrong.'

Peace with Jane

'No, you've got it all right,' said Gina. 'In any case we agreed that friends ought not to attempt to counsel each other as if they were amateur psychologists. But what you have said makes an awful lot of sense.

'I'm still not clear about how it causes this division between theory and practice, though, "private behaviour and public stance" as you said. And I don't see how I can get rid of it.'

'Well I can't answer all the questions,' said Margaret, 'but I think the first problem will be solved when you have dealt, or when the Lord has dealt, with the fear. There are two things to say, no three:

'One: you have seen and admitted the problem. That's a great point gained. I suggest we pray together about it in a minute and ask for God's healing of that particular hurt. Yes, you see I'm not as old-fashioned as you may have thought.

'Two: you have already broken one of the relationship barriers, if not two.'

'Really?' said Gina, wondering who was in mind.

'Well there's us, for one,' said Margaret with more warmth than grammatical accuracy, 'and Shelley.'

'You're right again, of course,' said Gina. 'What a blind fool I am. Here am I being so much afraid of people that I have been getting very close to one, to two, without noticing it. That *is* encouraging. Now, three.'

'Three is Jane I'm afraid,' said Margaret. 'As a sign that you mean to take the matter seriously I think you've got to go and see Jane and make things right with her.'

They prayed and they hugged and Gina visited Jane the next night and enjoyed the happiest evening she could remember. Jane and Gina established a relationship that grew and flourished, and although Gina continued to have problems of one kind or another she never again 'came a cropper' as Cyril had called it, and she opened her house to a new generation of friends.

Old Mrs Goodrich looked through the gap in the curtains and wondered...

'Shall I tell you what Mummy said?'

So in Gina's case the reasons for the gap between the public stance and the private behaviour (which had so unfortunately become public in the middle of the night) were complicated. She saw the need for her professed faith to be consistent with her actions, but was unable to cope with the stress.

Some of us are less complicated. We just do not acknowledge what we are really like. We deceive ourselves into thinking that we are pretty blameless on the whole (and are probably getting annoyed at the suggestion that we may not be, even as we read this, or are muttering in our minds, 'Well, this bit doesn't apply to me').

How often have you seen cars with Jesus stickers on them, exceeding the speed limit? Why do so many Christians seem to think that all laws should be kept except that one? James suggests that whoever breaks one law is guilty of breaking the lot (James 2:10). If you don't drive, think of your own example.

One of the most powerful deterrents against new people joining our churches is just this — Christians' private behaviour does not match their public stance. 'Hypocrites', they call us. Too often it's true. This is one of those contradictions which should *not* be there. The problem is that we like to pretend to others, even to ourselves, that it isn't, but if our friends and neighbours can see the inconsistencies, we may be sure that God can too.

After church one Sunday morning, Gordon and Margaret were counting the collection, and nearly everyone else had gone home. Timothy and Diana were talking to Shelley. Shelley was sitting on a pew, swinging her legs and glowing. Diana had just told her how nicely her teeth were growing.

'Mummy's helping Daddy counting the money,' said Shelley.

'Yes, isn't it nice that they help one another,' said Diana.

'You're very lucky to have parents who love each other so much and help each other like that,' said Timothy.

145

Shelley wrinkled up her nose.

'They don't always,' she said with conviction. 'The other day they had a fight. Shall I tell you what Mummy said?'

Diana and Timothy exchanged a hasty glance.

'No, Shelley. I don't think you'd better,' said Timothy.

Are you aware of the gap between stance and behaviour in other people?
How about yourself?
What can you do about either?

17

Peter and Cornelius

Simon the tanner's wife recovered fairly quickly from the shock of entertaining three extra for lunch (and one of them a Roman soldier), and Peter soon began to appreciate that Cornelius, their boss, was rather a special kind of person. A Gentile, of course, a Roman, but a pious one, in the best sense of the word; prayerful, benevolent and generous. It was clear that these men expected Peter to travel with them the thirty miles back to Caesarea and they believed that he had something very special to say to Cornelius.

What that special message was Peter did not know. This was turning out to be a very strange day. First the vision about unclean animals and now three men out of the blue asking him to go on a thirty-mile journey to an army camp to give a centurion some vital message which Peter had no clue about!

Well, when in God's service, don't hang about. Obey. The Spirit had told him to go with these men, so he went. Not that day (they were already tired) but the next, taking six Christians from Joppa with them. The little party made good progress over the day's ride, probably stayed the night at the home of one of Cornelius' servants ('Is my bed aired, Mum? Oh yes, and we need another nine') and did the last few miles to Caesarea the following morning. Two days on from the vision and Peter still had no idea what he was to say or whether the vision had anything to do with it.

Unclean people!

Meanwhile back at base, Cornelius was waiting for them. He reckoned that three days was about right for a sixty-mile journey and had collected his household, his relatives and his close friends and fellow officers. There was high excitement. Cornelius was a very steady, level-headed man. He would not stir up emotion without reason. Yet he was convinced that this man of God, Peter by name, had a vital message for them all. He did not have the slightest notion what it might be. But Peter would know.

Peter and his friends were admitted by the duty guard. Peter looked at Cornelius and Cornelius looked at Peter. There was a silence. No-one spoke. Then Cornelius suddenly prostrated himself at Peter's feet.

'Get up, man!' Peter was with him in a moment, helping him to his feet. 'I'm only a fellow man. I'm no more divine than this duty guard here.' The guard smiled sheepishly and then stood abruptly to attention as the centurion glared at him.

'No, I'm only a messenger. I've come because the Spirit of my God told me to come. And because you invited me. Now tell me what you want to know.'

Without a word Cornelius led Peter inside, to a hall packed with people. Unclean people! Not particularly smelly people (quite a relief from Joppa in fact) but ceremonially unclean. For a Jew to enter the house of a Gentile was against his religion. All these people crammed into the hall. It was like a...what did it remind him of? Like a sail-cloth full of unclean animals. So *that* was it! Do not call unclean what God calls clean. It was God's permission for him to visit them and talk to them.

All this passed through Peter's mind while Cornelius made a few introductory remarks. Still no clue as to what he was to say!

So Peter explained what he had just realized, that although as a faithful Jew he ought not to be with them, yet God had shown him that he should come in this case.

'So when I was sent for, I came without raising any objection. May I ask why you sent for me?'

Now Cornelius was on the spot. He still had no question to ask. If this man was really a man of God surely he'd *know* what God wanted him to say! A sudden fear came upon him. Suppose nothing came of all this. All these people! His reputation would be in tatters. Well, too late to think of that now. Here goes:

'Four days ago while I was praying at three in the after-noon' (he used the inclusive reckoning; this was now the fourth day of these events), 'a man in shining clothes stood before me' (those heathens won't understand me if I start talking about angels) 'and told me to send for Simon Peter. He gave me the exact address too. So I sent for you *at once*' (True. The three messengers did the thirty miles in about twenty hours, including an overnight stop) 'and it was good of you to come. Now here we all are, in the presence of God to hear what you have to say.'

'The Holy Spirit came'

Then it came to Peter in a moment of insight. Not only was God giving him permission to visit these people but, most staggering idea yet, to preach the good news, to share the gospel with them as well. 'Don't call unclean what God calls clean.'

So Peter stood up and spoke of the love of God in Christ, how Jesus had died for us all on the cross, and *all* now meant this group of non-Jews as well as the chosen people.

'While Peter was still speaking these words,' says Luke in Acts 10:44, 'the Holy Spirit came on all who heard the message.' They rejoiced, they praised God in their own language and in tongues. It was a vivid demonstration of the Spirit's work which astonished the Jewish Christians who had come with Peter. And Peter was already taking a further step:

'Can anyone keep these people from being baptized with water? They have received the Holy Spirit just as we have.'

They had repented and received the Spirit and were now baptized in water. All three requisites for true believers. In the wrong order, perhaps, but never mind that. The mystery was solved, the vision explained, the Jewish minds opened to the Gentile believers and there was great joy.

These events recorded in Acts 10 sum up more clearly than any other episode in the life of Peter exactly what this book, *The Simon Peter File*, is trying to say.

Here were two apparently mutually exclusive ideologies, the Jewish and the Roman. The Jews believed the Romans to be idolaters and blasphemers. The Romans saw the Jews as exclusivist fanatics.

Here were two groups of people, Peter and his friends, Cornelius and his entourage, both well-meaning, each ready to do what was expected of them by God, but both blinded by their background to the unity they might have enjoyed. The Romans despised the Christians' leader (they had crucified him), the Jews despised the Roman people (*goyim*).

But God had a plan. Neither of these groups could comprehend it. They obeyed God. Then they circled round each other, looking for an opening to know what God was saying. When at last they stumbled upon it together the Holy Spirit came in power, in demonstration of God's approval of what had happened.

So it is in many of our churches and so it was in Canwell Park. Groups of people, circling round each other, knowing very imperfectly what God is calling them to do, yet behind it all God does have a plan and God will work his purpose out as year succeeds to year.

Planners and pragmatists

Groups of people like these, especially religious people or those devoted to politics, frequently find it hard to understand one another because they approach life in different ways. We have met this problem in part with Fred and Timothy over the question of inspiration and preparation of sermons.

On the one hand are the planners, those who believe that life should be organized according to principles. They place, as it were, a wire mesh over the pattern of their life and try to live according to precise rules. The extreme example here is the Pharisees of our Lord's time who had a rule for almost everything they did. These extremists are legalistic. They will go to ridiculous lengths in order not to break the letter of their law. We are all familiar with examples such as the people, forbidden by their laws to travel over land on the Sabbath, who ride in cars great distances sitting on water bottles since they are now travelling over water!

But that is an extreme case, and to ridicule the extreme fanatic is a cheap way to rubbish a perfectly respectable idea — trying to make one's life conform to good and wise principles. For Christians this must surely be a very important matter. Moral principles (a clear idea of what is right and wrong); principles of daily living (disciplined use of time for prayer, Bible reading, worship, exercise, work, relaxation) and principles for the use of money (what proportion to spend, save, give to charity and so on) all these are surely admirable characteristics.

On the other hand we have the pragmatists, the people who act on the spur of the moment, who refuse to be tied down to a rigid plan. At worst these people are infuriatingly bizarre in their behaviour, conforming to no patterns at all and acting spontaneously and unpredictably. At best they are the geniuses with that bit of extra sparkle, that willingness to see things originally, that capacity for taking a risk, which are marks of brilliance.

In theory these two groups, the planners and the pragmatists, should be able to understand and make allowance for one another, to use each other's insights and change their own approach according to new wisdom observed in the others. The ideal man or woman must be the planned pragmatist or the pragmatic planner — one who can use the best of both approaches.

But there was only ever one ideal person. And he got crucified.

It looks easy. It looks as if all we need to do is to study the evidence and decide whether we would like to be planners or pragmatists and live accordingly. Then if we find it not working out we can change systems. And we would all understand each other because we would all be thinking and feeling the same way.

Unfortunately it doesn't work like that. We don't choose to be planners. We follow our temperament. The planner-by-nature finds it very hard to become spontaneous and to break his rules 'for once'. Ask a person who has carefully saved a specific percentage of his income for many years to fly with you to the Bahamas next week 'for a lark' and see what response you get.

And because we plan or refuse to plan according to our temperament, we find it difficult to enter into the feelings of those who do things differently. We try to understand each other but we can't really feel what they feel.

If these two characteristics are polarized in a married couple — a planner married to a pragmatist — there is often big trouble in getting along together. She wants a surprise treat. He wants to plan it weeks in advance. Or he announces a trip to France tomorrow, but she needs time to get her hair done, see to Auntie, write ten letters, put the cat in the cattery — and what about the list of jobs to be done at the weekend?

Some like it cool; some like it hot;
Some freeze while others smother.
And by some fatal, fiendish plot,
They marry one another.

'A political dinosaur'

It's hard enough for people to understand one another, even when they *want* to. Very often they don't want to.

Have you ever heard politicians arguing in public and really trying to understand each other's point of view? It must be a rare phenomenon. Usually it's more like this:

A: 'My honourable friend has already referred to his party's record in office. His own and his party's record is one of vacillation, confusion and broken pledges. They have done U-turns and W-turns. They have no policy at all and stick to it.'

B: 'Of course we have not followed a rigid, dogmatic strait-jacket policy. We are a party of *today*. We respond to new ideas. We are alive and move with the times. We observe the winds of change and cut our cloth to suit the weather. To be a political dinosaur like my honourable friend here, is to court extinction in today's rapidly moving world.'

A: 'My honourable friend accuses me and my party of being dinosaurs and talks of extinction. That is merely his debased way of referring to our honourable record of faithfulness to our principles, yes sir, principles, which we believe in and which we will not abandon with every puff of economic or political breeze...'

And so on and so forth, each blinding himself to the positive value of his opponent's position, be it flexibility or be it faithfulness to known values, and each accusing the other of the negative aspect of his approach, vacillation or rigidity.

'I am firm. He is stubborn. You are pig-headed.'

Is there no hope for us then? Are we all at the mercy

of our inclination to be planners or pragmatists, sombre or spontaneous?

Yes there is hope. It is possible to understand and work well with someone of a different temperament. In fact it can be a wonderfully stimulating experience. We shall never be perfect but, in Christ and by the power of the Holy Spirit, temperaments can merge in a powerfully creative manner.

Are you a planner? Or a pragmatist?
Which would you rather be?
How can you enrich your life by being better planned — or more spontaneous?
Be specific.

18

Reconciliation

I t was 7.45 on a Sunday evening. The members of St Barnabas' Church had enjoyed an 'ordinary' service for once. No ancient prayer book, no healing, no counselling, no special items, just a straightforward service of worship with a thought-provoking but not very passionate sermon from the vicar. In fact Timothy felt that it had all fallen rather flat.

As the final hymn drew to a close he reflected that only one unusual thing had occurred — Connie Bassett had come to the service. Since the healing service little Mabel had been a regular attender with Mrs Beesley but Connie had usually stayed away. Now her great form could be seen occupying half a pew towards the back of the church.

A movement caught Timothy's eye. Connie was heaving

herself out of her place. 'Off early, I suppose,' thought Timothy, 'she doesn't want to have to talk to anyone in case they try to get her converted.'

But Connie was not making for the door. She was advancing steadily up the centre aisle with a rhythmic roll, like a great ship at sea. She reached the steps in front of the astonished vicar and knelt with some difficulty on the floor in front of him.

'Lay yer 'ands on me, reverend,' she said in a hoarse whisper.

'But it's not a counselling service or a healing service,' Timothy heard himself saying.

'No, but it's a *Christian* service ain't it?' said Connie. 'I've just give me 'eart to Jesus like you said, so I need the 'oly Ghost to 'elp me change a bit.'

There was complete silence as Timothy stepped forward, laid his hands on Connie's head and prayed that the Holy Spirit would come into her life and stay there.

Connie rose up, climbed the two steps and faced the congregation, her face radiant.

'It's 'appened,' she said. 'It's 'appened even to me. All those years since Canon George 'ealed me, well all right, since Gawd 'ealed me, I've been running away. And now I want to tell you what's made me stop running. I'm too fat to run for one thing.' (Polite titters from some.) 'But it's Mrs Beesley what's to blame. She's been such a good friend to me. And she never preached at me. She took me to the outing at Littlehampton and I *did* enjoy it.

'Then Mr Jenkins, 'e wanted to sing choruses and Mr Barber 'e wanted to sing something else and they was both so *nice* about it afterwards. I thought, "there's something going on 'ere".

'Then I came to the 'ealing service and Mabel's arthritis

got better. There's certainly something going on.

'So I want you all to know that I've stopped running away from Jesus and I've turned round and run into 'is arms and I'm sorry for all I've done wrong. Now I've believed in 'im and I've received the Spirit as well. The other thing is baptism ain't it? Well I've never been done so it's time I was. But I want to go in properly. That font won't hold me, will it?' She turned a bright eye on Timothy.

Her rich Cockney guffaw filled the church. It broke the tension and a great gale of laughter swept the congregation, not because what Connie had said was particularly funny but because they were all so happy.

Chalk meets cheese

'So,' said Connie, 'I'll see you all at the swimming baths behind the fire station and we'll do it proper.'

She clambered down the steps to a spontaneous burst of applause. Timothy suggested that they should all sing 'Praise God from whom all blessings flow', which they did, several times, and the service was over.

Timothy made his way through the small crowd surrounding Connie and shook her warmly by the hand. But this was not what Connie had in mind. She opened her arms wide and enveloped him completely in a great bear-hug, from which he emerged breathless and rather dishevelled.

'What about the baptism then?' said Connie, 'will next week do?'

'I think we ought to have a few talks together first,' said Timothy. 'We always have instruction classes for adult baptism. You need to think it all through you know. There's a lot to learn.'

'I'll bet there is,' said Connie. 'All them 'ezekiahs and Hisaiahs and Gawd knows who. Well all right, let's keep the rules. But I'll not take lessons from you, young man. I thank God your sermon gave me the push I needed. But I want advice from someone nearer me own age.'

She looked about her and her eye fell on Cyril Kent who was hovering at the edge of the group, pretending not to be there.

'Mr Kent now, he'll do,' said Connie decidedly.

'Me? Oh dear no,' said Cyril hastily, 'I'm sure the vicar...'

'You heard what the lady said,' said Timothy, sensing the irony of the situation. 'You *are* an elder. You are quite well qualified to lead a baptism candidate through the basics of the faith.'

'And you was 'ealed, so I 'eard.' This carried much more weight with Connie than qualifications to discuss doctrine.

'Well, yes, er no, well not exactly,' stammered Cyril as Connie advanced on him. Terrified that she would attempt to hug him, he dodged behind the bookstall and conducted the rest of the conversation from relative safety.

Finally Cyril agreed to accept Connie as a candidate for a baptism class, though he insisted that his wife Edith should take part as well ('very proper too,' Connie had said) and asked for at least six weekly meetings.

To the amazement of everyone, except perhaps of Connie herself, who never bothered to see difficulties in any situation ('I need all me strength to get about with,' she said, 'I've got no breath left to look for problems'), they got on remarkably well. The conservative, upright Cyril, who loved the Authorized Version of the Bible and the Book of Common Prayer and who acted very 'correctly' on all occasions was confronted with a huge Cockney woman with a very wide vocabulary, who had sung in night

159

clubs and public houses and who spoke with a very loud voice. 'Chalk meets cheese' said some, yet the friendship between the Kents and Connie Bassett flourished and they benefited enormously from each other's company.

Sure of her new convictions, Connie, of course, let everyone know about them. The residents of 'The Haven' were left in no doubt that something very wonderful had happened to her — though some of the older residents were confused as to what it was.

They were all invited to the baptism, which did take place in the swimming baths behind the fire station (in the shallow end). Huge numbers of people turned up, including most of the (mobile) residents of 'The Haven' and a large contingent from the Canwell Christian Fellowship as well as members of the Baptist and Methodist churches too. The singing, in the echoing confines of the baths, was magnificent.

Reconciliation had taken place between Connie and her Maker and had spread to Cyril and Edith, several members of 'The Haven' community, and now even brought together Christians from four of the denominational groups in the area. In later months and years Connie was to introduce many of her friends to her best friend, as she called him, 'you know, Jesus'. Her conversion was just the kind of gift that God surprises his people with when they least expect it.

Progress, but not perfection

The light that was gradually, oh so gradually, dawning over St Barnabas', Canwell Park showed people to each other as real brothers and sisters rather than representatives of differing points of view. Gina and Jane would perhaps never agree about how the Holy Spirit works, but they could find joy in getting to know each other's problems and weaknesses and strengths and *accepting* each other.

The Holy Spirit worked at St Barnabas' in other totally unexpected ways. The 'progressives' expected renewal in what they saw as a normal manner — more and more people experiencing baptism in the Spirit, culminating in the vicar joining their ranks, and the revolution of worship in spontaneity and joy, with tongues, prophecy and healing. The 'conservatives' had been praying that God (they did not mention the Third Person of the Trinity) would curb excesses, keep them all secure in their traditional forms of worship and defend their vicar from emotional experiences. And, if possible, that the 'progressives' would leave their church and join the Canwell Christian Fellowship where they clearly belonged.

In fact a few people did leave St Barnabas'. About fifteen altogether. A few joined the CCF because the pace of renewal at St Barnabas' was too slow. A few joined St Augustine's, Canford Heath, because, although it was 'high church', at least you knew where you were with Father Aubrey. A few others ceased to come to church at all and satisfied their consciences with 'Songs of Praise' on the telly.

So neither side 'won'. The services remained a mixture of choruses and traditional hymns, freedom and structure, organ and guitar, prayer book and free prayer. Nobody thought that it was ideal. The whole thing seemed like a bit of a compromise. Some complained that it was the worst of all worlds because nobody was completely satisfied. But the Spirit of God was teaching them all that love is more important than a guitar or an organ. Forgiveness is wider than a chorus or a psalm. Concern for your brother or sister's welfare stands higher in God's sight than a prayer book, or absence of a prayer book. Paul's teaching on love

161

in 1 Corinthians 13 is at the heart of what he says about worship in chapters 12 and 14.

So the Spirit crept up on them all and took them by surprise. Some wouldn't recognize what he was doing but there was a very gradual easing of tension and opening of windows to what God could do, despite his people! And more than one believed that it had begun with Fred and Gordon shaking hands on the pavement after the trip to Littlehampton. They remembered too that it had been Connie Bassett who had been instrumental in bringing them together. God had a strange sense of humour it seemed.

Neither did everyone become perfect. Connie came to church regularly but her language still left something to be desired for a long time. Mrs Beesley continued to annoy Timothy by telling him how good Canon George had been. Against all outward appearances Gordon and Margaret did have some differences which Shelley was quick to observe.

But then, as we noticed before, Peter was not perfect either. Even after Pentecost. Those who believe that he was raised above reproach that day at nine o'clock in the morning should perhaps look again at Galatians 2.

'He was wrong'

Paul speaking, or rather writing:

> *When Peter came to Antioch, I opposed him*
> *to his face because he was in the wrong*
> (Galatians 2:11).

Strong words from one great apostle about another. Why was Paul so upset?

It seemed that Peter had been putting into practice the

principles that he was learning, that all people are equal before God and that Jewish Christians might have full fellowship with Gentile Christians.

Then a party of hard-liners from the church in Jerusalem had been sent to check up on what was going on. What would Peter do? Hold fast to the convictions that he had come to believe in, or give way to pressure from the ecclesiastical powers that were? He gave way. He withdrew from the Gentiles in order to satisfy the authorities. This was wrong, says Paul. It was more, it was hypocrisy. And it was hypocrisy which caused others to slide sideways into error, including the faithful Barnabas himself.

'You are a Jew,' thundered Paul to Peter, 'yet you live like a Gentile and not like a Jew.'

Peter, you've let the side down. Again. Here you were filled with the Spirit, used to work miracles, a courageous preacher, standing up in public and boldly defying the government, yet when you were stared at by the dignitaries of the church you collapsed like a pack of cards and turned your back on your brothers in Christ to keep level with the party line. Oh Peter! Call yourself a member of the Chosen Race? You're acting like an outcast.

'No, Lord, no. It's against my religion...'

What a muddle.

No, Peter was never perfect. Tradition has it that at the end of his life he fled from Rome when persecution threatened. He found his way barred by the Lord himself. '*Quo vadis, domine?*' he said, 'Where are you going Lord?'

'To Rome,' replied Jesus, 'To be crucified again in your place.'

Peter is said to have turned back shamefaced, to meet Nero and his own crucifixion.

Perhaps Paul had this possibility in mind as he rebuked

163

Peter in the second chapter of Galatians, and incidentally he introduced yet another of the mysteries, another 'both/and'. The true Christian is both alive and dead:

> *I have been crucified with Christ and I no longer live, but Christ lives in me. The life I live in the body, I live by faith in the Son of God, who loved me and gave himself for me* (Galatians 2:20).

Wrong, yet justified; vibrantly alive, yet crucified; defeated yet victorious. Who can understand these things? Perhaps we don't need to understand them, but to accept them with thankfulness.

Is God really as powerful as this chapter has suggested, in your experience?
And is he really so untidy?
Would you prefer it if he were more predictable?

19

Living with enrichment

Timothy Monteith grasped the handle of his front door and opened it with a prayer of thanksgiving. He walked with a light tread across the car park to the church hall. The church council was to meet at 7.45.

He remembered, as he walked the fifty yards or so, another occasion, only a few months previously, when he had wished to be anywhere but among these hostile people, all demanding different things. Yet now, though very little had changed outwardly, a great internal revolution had come to St Barnabas' and it was with pleasurable anticipation that Timothy opened the hall door to prepare for the meeting.

Where do you put your books?

Nothing demonstrated this revolution more simply or dramatically than the grouping of the council members as they made their way to the hall.

Gina Holwell was, for once, not walking briskly. She was measuring her pace to the slow, literally painfully slow, progress of Jane Goodrich. Gina was discovering that Jane had some very good reasons for wanting to retain pews in the church. After services, those who wanted coffee, but got tired of standing, needed somewhere to put their cups. If there were people on either side of you, you couldn't put your cup on a seat. You needed a ledge — a good wide one. Similarly during the service, you needed somewhere for your hymn book, Bible, prayer book, glasses. And if (here Jane looked archly at Gina) you wanted to put your hymn book down to clap, what did you do with it? Put it on your own seat? Then you forgot it was there and sat on it...

The discussion continued animatedly but both Jane and Gina were being constructive, respecting one another, as they never had before, and ready to learn from what the other said.

Ahead of them, in Highwood Avenue, Gordon, Margaret and Fred were walking, rather more quickly, towards the church hall. The rift between Fred and Gordon over the Littlehampton bus affair had long been healed and they were back on their old easy terms of friendship. Margaret, as will have been noticed, had come a long way towards the 'progressives'' point of view in the past few months and was beginning to see that Fred was not the hare-brained fanatic she had taken him for. He was delighted to discover how deeply Margaret had become involved in the counselling and healing ministries.

Moreover, they were getting excited about a compromise plan for the alteration of the church interior which they thought might please most people and be a much better solution than the 'leave-it-as-it-is' or 'tear-it-all-apart' suggestions so far put forward.

Meanwhile Cyril Kent's car was drawing up in the car park. Timothy saw it arrive as he glanced through the hall window. Cyril got out and walked round to the passenger door. Timothy could see only the back of the car from where he was sitting. The car rocked to and fro and suddenly a guffaw of laughter rent the air. Connie Bassett! Surely she wasn't coming to the meeting! She wasn't an elected member of the council. Timothy supposed she could come as an observer, with no voting rights of course, if she could keep quiet, but he knew that she wouldn't be able to. He got up and looked out of the window.

An extraordinary sight met his eyes. Connie Bassett and Cyril Kent apparently involved in a wrestling match, trying to prize Connie out of the car, and both helpless with mirth. Timothy watched in amazement. Connie was finally extracted and dusted and set on her feet.

'Are you sure you don't want a lift the rest of the way?' asked Cyril hesitantly.

'What, and 'ave to go through all that again?' said Connie. 'No fear. I mean no thanks, dear. It's only an 'undred yards down the road.'

Timothy blinked as Cyril opened his arms and gave Connie a farewell hug.

At the same moment, Margaret, Gordon and Fred came round the corner.

'The wolf and the lamb shall feed together,' said Gordon quietly. 'Wonders never cease.'

God above us

The atmosphere was warm and positive. There was a freedom in the meeting which no-one could remember experiencing before. Jokes were exchanged and there was a lot of banter, but all in a good spirit.

Timothy announced that before the decision was to be made concerning the church furniture there would be a time for prayer. There was general approval for this, but before the prayer began Fred asked if he might say a few words.

'Before we discuss anything, I want to apologize to everyone for being so pig-headed' (cries of 'No, Fred' and 'Don't exaggerate'). 'No, I mean it. I've not considered anyone else's feelings and I've said some hurtful things. I think we all need to get that out of the way before we begin.

'I think God spoke to us about this when we went on holiday. We were on the night ferry, leaving Harwich. It was a lovely calm evening and the lights were reflected on the water, and I said, "Those lights are really lovely you know." Then Joan, you know Joan, she's always down to earth, she says, "The water's pretty filthy I expect." And Carol, she says, "It's just like the church isn't it? All bright and sparkling on the surface, but the light's reflecting off some murky substance." Those were her words, "murky substance". And she was right. The light is from God and it looks beautiful but underneath we've all been a bit murky haven't we?'

He sat down.

Timothy stood up. 'Fred,' he said, 'I believe you're right. God has spoken to you and to us all by that illustration. Let's pray now with that picture in mind.'

Then, one after another, the members of the council asked forgiveness for their lack of sensitivity to each other and their selfishness in demanding their own way. Timothy had to break in, after fifteen minutes, as the prayer threatened to take up more time than the discussion. When they were ready to discuss, the feeling was one of anticipation and readiness to co-operate.

Gordon Barber was called up to propose a way forward. He had his visual aids ready and switched on the overhead projector.

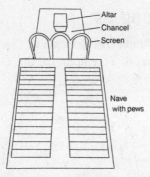

'When these churches were designed in the Middle Ages,' said Gordon, 'they were intended to draw attention to the holy place, the altar at the east end where mass was celebrated. In fact it was so holy that a screen was probably erected to separate the chancel from the body of the church where the common worshippers were.

'We think this sounds awful, but they had one good point. God is holy. God is above us all. He is, to use the technical term "transcendent", beyond us and worthy of all our awe and respect. The concept of the altar at the east end underlines God's otherness and special holiness.

'The screen went at the Reformation and we call the

altar the holy table now, but we still express the idea of
going up to visit a holy God, who has mercy on us, when
we walk up to receive bread and wine at communion. As
far as it goes this is good.

'But we have understood more recently that God is not
only transcendent but he is also immanent...'

'He's swallowed the Bible dictionary,' said Fred.

'Order, order,' called Timothy. The laughter died down
and Gordon proceeded.

God among us

'Immanent. Among us. Between us. "In the midst", as the
old phrase has it. To emphasize this element of worship

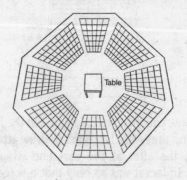

a different-shaped church is often built today, octagonal
or round, with the table in the middle. Chairs or pews are
grouped round to lead the eye naturally to the centre. To
receive bread and wine, worshippers stand in a ring round
the table or pass the loaf and cup round to each other.
The Bible is read from the centre, the sermon is preached
from there and so the three emphases are literally central, the word written, the word preached and the Word

sacrificed for us which we remember at the Lord's supper.

'Now that's fine, but *our* building is the wrong shape. But the plan we are proposing takes care of that too.'

Gordon changed to his third acetate.

'The idea is that we can get the best of both worlds. We can curtain off the chancel and place the holy table in the centre. So we have the nearest thing to a church in the round, emphasizing God's nearness and centrality. When we want to remind ourselves of his transcendence, his holiness and power, we can open the curtain and use the old position of the table as before.

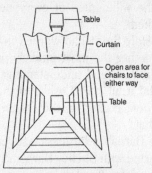

'Fixed pews will be ranged round three sides — we can use the ones we've got, so there's only the expense of moving some of them — chairs can be used at the front to face whichever way we want. The old chancel can be used for drama or whatever else we like and it can be curtained off, thus saving on heating bills.

'The pulpit and the reading desk will be movable so they can face either way.

'I place before the council this suggestion, which the sub-committee has been working on, as a theologically meaningful, reasonably cheap solution which ought to please most people when and if we are prepared to get used to it.'

Gordon sat down and dabbed his bald head with a handkerchief. The applause died down and the questions began. Some adjustments were made and some objections debated, but it seemed that the whole idea chimed in with the desire for an arrangement that would suit traditionalists and progressives.

When Timothy described the progress of the meeting to Diana later that evening they both agreed that it was not the details of the arrangement of the chairs that mattered but the willingness of everyone to co-operate in arranging them.

God the Holy Spirit had worked in unexpected ways, bringing together the most unlikely people and stirring up a spirit of love and understanding.

'Where did it all start?' asked Diana.

'With Connie Bassett in the coach?'

'Before that.'

'With the Barnabas business last year?' said Timothy. 'That all started with Shelley Barber drawing a picture in Sunday School for Gordon.'

'I think a lot of this change has come through your sermons on Simon Peter you know. And where did that idea come from?'

'Gordon. At least, no, not Gordon, Gordon got it from Shelley! Shelley Barber again. I think she'd better take over this church. It's too complicated for me.'

Shelley Barber again

Gordon and Margaret were not surprised to hear running footsteps upstairs as soon as the baby-sitter had gone. As usual the white-clad figure appeared on the stairs.

'Now then poppet,' said Gordon. 'I suppose you want to know everything that happened at the meeting.'

'No,' said Shelley, settling herself on his knee, 'I think meetings are boring. I'd rather watch "Top of the Pops".'

Margaret raised her eyes to the ceiling. 'Seven', was all she could say.

'Is that what you've been doing while we were out?'

'Yes. "The Infernal Body-Blow Machine" came straight in at number twenty-three.'

'I'm impressed,' said Gordon very seriously.

'While you were watching "Top of the Pops" the council was discussing Daddy's new plan to change the church,' said Margaret.

'Oh,' said Shelley.

'And nearly everyone agreed about it. It will be a lovely church and all the people will be friendly again. You were saying that people were nasty to each other. I don't think they will be any more.'

'Oh,' said Shelley.

'And you had something to do with that, because you said Simon Peter was a blundering buffoon and we ought to think about him. So we did and it helped us all.'

'Oh', said Shelley again.

'Is that all you can say, "Oh"?'

Shelley gave a deep sigh.

'I don't think I can wait till next Thursday,' she said.

'Why next Thursday?' asked Margaret, but Gordon could see it coming.

'Because I expect "The Infernal Body-Blow Machine" will be on again. He's *fab*ulous. Carol says so.'

'That *child*,' said Margaret after Shelley had gone to bed for the second time.

173

'Well, she keeps everything in perspective for us,' said Gordon laughing. ' "The Infernal Body-Blow Machine" and "Blundering buffoons". Good grief!'

What shape is your church building and how is it arranged?
How does it help you to worship God?
In the light of eternity is the furniture *so* important?

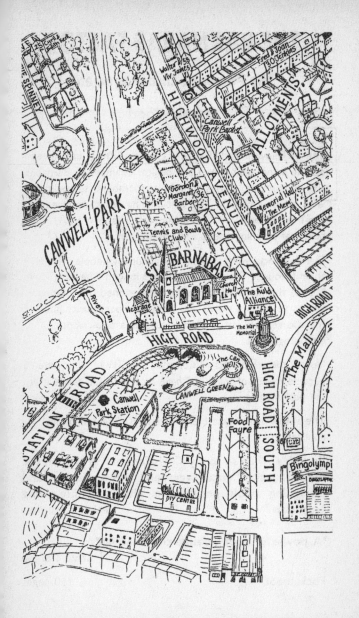

THE BARNABAS FACTOR

The Power of Encouragement

Derek Wood

Life at Canwell Park Church, London SW31, can never
be the same again when the biblical example of Barnabas,
the encourager, begins to grip its members, sometimes
with amusing results. This fast-moving book interweaves
the lives of ordinary Christians with effective and
practical teaching about encouragement.

Derek Wood writes: 'Ask any group of people who is
their favourite Bible character and it won't be long
before the name of Barnabas is mentioned. He comes
across to us as a warm and attractive personality and,
for this reason, is the ideal focus for a book about
encouragement.

'As for the inhabitants of Canwell Park, SW31, they have all
become friends of mine as I have recorded their doings over
the past months.'

The result is a unique blend of storytelling and biblical
application.

**'In a day when so many Christians are drying on the
vine for lack of encouragement, this fascinating and
intriguing book provides a vital and life-giving
emphasis.'** *Selwyn Hughes*

'A powerful book...dangerous reading!'
Clive Calver

Pocketbook   160 pages